For the Love of Books

A Guide to Help Teachers Connect Middle Grade Readers with Literature

by
Jane M. Vossler

National Middle School Association
Westerville, Ohio

National Middle School Association
4151 Executive Parkway, Suite 300
Westerville, Ohio 43081
(800) 528-NMSA

Sue Swaim, Executive Director
Jeff Ward, Associate Executive Director
Edward Brazee, Editor, Professional Publications
John Lounsbury, Consulting Editor, Professional Publications
Mary Mitchell, Designer, Copy Editor
Marcia Meade-Hurst, Senior Publications Representative
Sara Levengood, Production Manager
Kim Smith, Cover Design

Illustrations by students of Jane Vossler

Library of Congress Cataloging-in-Publication Data
Vossler, Jane.
   For the love of books : a guide to help teachers connect middle
   grade readers with literature / byJane M. Vossler.
      p. cm.
   ISBN 1-56090-132-2
      1. Middle school students--Books and reading--United States. 2. Preteens--Books and reading--United States. 3. Young adult literature, American--Stories, plots, etc. 4. Young adult literature, American--Study and teaching (Middle school)--United States. 5. Self-perception--Juvenile literature--Bibliography. 6. Difference (Psychology)--Juvenile literature--Bibliography. 7. Toleration--Juvenile literature--Bibliography. I. National Middle School Association. II. Title.

Z1037.A1 V67 2002
028.5'35--dc21   2002033666

With heartfelt thanks

...to my mother who taught me to love reading

...to my husband, Larry Hills,
for his patient critiques and endless encouragement,

...and to all the Odyssey team students who over the years
have shared with me their lives, views of the world,
and thoughts about literature.

They all made this book possible.

Contents

Foreword

I learned to read the summer I was 12, and it changed my life forever.

In elementary school I had managed to sight-read and decode new words, but as I recall that meant little more to me than performing other cognitive gymnastics like spelling and reciting multiplication tables – proficiencies to be demonstrated and then set aside in favor of the stuff that really mattered to a small town southern boy in the 1940s, things like playing ball, and chasing cats, and biking with my pals. And as long as teachers didn't agitate me too much with their insistence on such irrelevancies as abstract analyses of phonetics or the rules of grammar, I got along just fine without thinking very much about what I was doing.

I can't recall if some event significant at the time changed my thinking. Stories were important throughout my growing up years.

- anecdotes by professional baseball player cousins of living in hotels and traveling on trains and playing my beloved game before thousands of people
- my grandmother's accounts of growing up on a farm a few miles away in Hickory Flat with only her dog, Buddy, for a playmate
- ancient and blind Mr. Shanks' rocking chair stories about caring for Nathan Bedford Forrest's Confederate cavalry horses when he was a boy my age
- our neighbor Duddy Roark's spell-binding descriptions of soldiering in Europe and being in an advanced platoon that stumbled upon a German concentration camp
- listening to my favorite radio program in bed late at night, "You Were There," an aural reenactment of historic events spoken in dialogue that made me feel like I was indeed there

Since no distinct incident "grew me up," perhaps it was the gradually emerging consciousness of a young adolescent boy that there's a whole lot more to living than just hanging out.

Fifty years later I can't recall what we did at school in my junior high years, not even a single lesson. But I easily remember the more than a dozen books and authors I read in my tree house during the heat of those summer days when I was 12.

- Clair Bee's riveting fiction series about Chip Hilton and his sidekick, Speedy Morris
- Mark Twain's immortal *Huckleberry Finn* that provoked my pals and me to build a cumbersome log raft on a neighborhood pond
- *The First Shot for Liberty* by an author whose name is now lost to me that recounted the resistance of French boys my age in the Great War
- that amazing *Being Born* that Pop gave me which when dropped to the floor would immediately fall open to page 31 with its stunning single paragraph about "doing it" (even today I can almost recite that entire paragraph from memory)
- Alfred Leland Crabb's compelling saga of the divided Carter Family in the middle of the 19th century told through a dozen volumes including *Dinner at Belmont, Supper at the Maxwell House, Home to Tennessee,* and *A Mockingbird Sang at Chickamauga*
- Erich Maria Remarque's still disturbing *All Quiet on the Western Front*

My heart skips as I list these titles and even more books from the last 50 years flood my mind. Processing the issues encountered in this mass of literature along with our actual lives was left to me and my pals, Brad and Little Jack. We knew we were dealing with heavy-duty stuff, but we had only each other to sort it out. Back then issues of sexuality, racial discrimination, relationships, friendship, secrets, duplicity, forgiveness, self-discovery, and the insecurities of neo-adolescent boys were not matters we directly talked about with grown-ups.

Where were you then when I needed you, Jane Vossler?

My teachers were nice enough, to be sure – well-meaning people who I'm sure believed they were doing the right things. But while nice was important, it was not nearly enough even back then, much less today. I understand now that my teachers were mostly anachronistic, assigning suspect importance to things that missed what really mattered in my life: ourselves as kids and our town and its people; our confusions about segregation and unfairness and what to believe about a God worshiped in racially segregated churches; sorrow and death when we lost my beloved grandfather, Doc; the excitement of vicarious adventure as many of our local men left on a troop train headed to Korea when President Truman called up the Dixie Division of the National Guard; unspoken questions and confusion when some of them soon returned in caskets; friendship, conflict, betrayal, and – of course – girls and love and the "s" word.

Jane Vossler and many other contemporary middle level educators understand and daily demonstrate as she has done in this superb volume that young adolescents have huge ideas and questions and priorities that constitute an all-too-often untapped mother-lode for teachers. Jim Beane has long urged us to acknowledge this obvious truth by building curriculum around youngsters' questions, issues, and ideas. Vossler's new book stands as an exceptionally useful guide to responding to kids' issues by drawing upon the plethora of excellent literature available today.

A conspicuous strength of this book is its use of inquiry to create the kind of openly questioning and trusting context that young adolescents can use to blur distinctions between problems introduced by literary plots and subplots and those that are actual in their own lives. "What would you do?" invites every reader (and teacher) to imagine all possible responses to a problem and in the safety of the discussion to extract ethical principles as well as personal reflections. Jane Vossler is savvy to the dynamic and diverse cognition of early adolescence and the power of youngsters' reflections and ethical choices. Every middle level teacher, from neophyte to veteran, who recognizes the intensity of kids' lives in the middle years will acclaim the propriety of this book's organization of literature into an interactive dichotomy of "Inner World" and "Outer World." And like the Cracker Jacks we loved in my generation, each chapter includes a prize: "Teaching Ideas" that enhance the sweetness of the literature itself.

Several years ago Jane wrote a brief piece for the Vermont Association for Middle Level Education (VAMLE) about a tradition in her partner team she titled "Parents and Kids Read Together." In it she explained how periodically throughout the school year her students and their parents would come to the team rooms for an evening hour's exchange about books they were reading *together*. The students would plan the agenda and prepare refreshments ahead. Time was given over to talk about books and authors in the same ways that are familiar to adults in book groups. What could be better than having each of one's students and one or both of the parents reading the same book together at the same time and *talking about it*? Imagine the impact on everyone present as one student and his or her parents talk about *Where the Red Fern Grows*; could there be a dry eye, an untouched heart in the house? Drawing on her considerable expertise inveigling students and parents to read and talk about text together, the author has included an excellent appendix of generic "Discussion Questions" for parents and teachers.

Teachers, regardless of their academic preferences, still read and enjoy a variety of literature. I wonder why it is, then, that for the most part middle level schools are organized so that only language arts teachers teach literature? This disjunction smacks of sex education courses taught only by the school nurse. Certainly every middle level language arts teacher will benefit from reading and using this volume. But if only they use it, an extraordinarily useful potential will be wasted. A goal worthy of every middle level school is to have everyone of every age and school responsibility *reading* and *talking* about their reading *together*. In the 1970s when I was a middle level teacher, I was reading Peter Benchley's *Jaws*. I offered to read it aloud to my students if they would complete their classroom clean-up and preparation for leaving quickly enough to leave us 15 minutes or so at the end of the day. They became so intensely interested in this routine that after a week or so they proposed that they would stay a half-hour after school on certain days if I would agree to continue the reading. Often teachers in schools with teacher advisory programs complain about having to come up with additional curriculum for advisory sessions. Well, folks, here is a terrific opportunity! I'd like to believe that once teachers have interacted with their advisees around the content of literature Vossler has reviewed in this volume, they will become more aware and sensitive to issues in their students' lives. And, of course, the ultimate benefit is that their interpersonal communication will be substantially improved, and teachers' effectiveness will be enhanced. Don't miss out!

Reading is a distinct intimacy – an engagement of mind and soul between thinkers. All people, from early childhood and continuing throughout their lives, are drawn to stories. My two-year-old granddaughter implores, "Read me a story, Doc"; my 88-year-old mother, whose conversational attention span has shrunk to fifteen seconds at best, still listens happily to anecdotes told from our present lives. Whatever else adults may do with and for their middle school students, nothing holds the potential for endurance that a love of reading and literature holds. These pages present an abundance of insight and tested pedagogy about how we can nurture and enhance this potential in young adolescents. And in ourselves, too.

Chris Stevenson
Professor Emeritus, University of Vermont
Pinehurst, North Carolina

*Books are magical, stupendous, marvelous, absolutely
wonderful, amazing, incredible, beautiful, educational,
and my best friends.* — Leah Marvin Riley, Grade 6

Introduction

My mother calls from the kitchen, "Jane, why don't you go outside for awhile. All you ever do is read." It's the middle of my 13th summer, and I sit curled up in an overstuffed chair. We made our weekly trip to the public library yesterday, so there's a tall pile of books on the table beside me. I hope it's enough to last me until our next trip.

In my mind I'm far away from the small, rural town in Connecticut where I've spent my entire life. I'm in colonial Massachusetts watching an angry crowd gather around the *Witch of Blackbird Pond.* Yesterday I was on Prince Edward Island with my friend, *Ann of Green Gables.*

Drawing by Mari Huessy

"Okay, Ma," I call back. I have no intention, of course, of leaving Kit and the witch just as things are getting exciting. The only thing that might make me stir is the arrival of the mail. Then I'd rush out to see if the latest copy of *American Girl* had come. This magazine carried stories by Betty Cavanna, romantic adventures of teenage girls that I waited impatiently for each month.

When I finished a book, I wrote a short summary of it on an index card and filed it alphabetically in a metal box. Unfortunately, sometime over the years, the box was lost. I'd give anything to be able to flip through those cards today and see what books were shaping my adolescent mind. But I have a pretty good idea what kind of books they were. Many were books with characters who took a chance, fought hard for what they believed in, and pursued their dreams. As I got older and read more sophisticated books I came to know characters intimately who were different from the limited circle of people – small town, middle class, white – I met in my daily life. People from different countries, of different races, with different beliefs and life stories. The rich and powerful. The poor and oppressed. Blacks and Native Americans. Refugees and the abused. I saw life through many different lens.

Books helped to shape the person I am today.

Thousands of books and a number of years of teaching brought me to Essex Middle School in the small, suburban community of Essex, Vermont. For the past fifteen years I've taught language arts and social studies to sixth, seventh, and eighth graders on a two-person team.

I want books to open up new worlds for my students, too. I want them to stretch beyond the limits, whatever those may be, of family and community, to get to know people who look different and think differently. I want them to imagine life in another country and in another person's skin. I want them to develop compassion for those who are less fortunate than they. I want them to see other ways of relating to each other, other dreams they never imagined. I want them to get the reading habit so they'll become lifelong lovers of literature who never stop reading, learning, growing. I know that books can do all these things if you open your mind and heart to them.

I hope this book will help you to help your students select good books. I hope you can feel the magic of connecting the right student with the right book. "How'd you like it?" you'll ask. "It was great! I want another one just like it," the student will reply. I hope this book will give you ideas for book discussions so your students can experience the intellectual excitement that comes from a lively exchange of ideas about books and the lives they contain. And most importantly, I hope it will inspire you to read more books yourself.

Happy Reading!

PART I: THE INNER WORLD

Books to help students think about themselves and their own lives

Albert Einstein said, "The world is too dangerous to live in – not because of the people who do evil, but because of the people who stand by and let them." The world would be a better place if we noticed the little acts of intolerance and spoke out against them. I know that one person really can make a difference. — Michael Jacobs, Grade 7

Chapter 1: Against the Tide
— Novels about standing up and speaking out —

Recently, my students and I studied World War II. An expert on the Holocaust from the university came to speak. He told of the gradual steps that Hitler took to identify, deport, and, finally, exterminate the Jews. Step by step, one law and then another until they had no rights left. At the end of this compilation of horror, the speaker asked, "How can you make sure this doesn't happen again?" His own answer was, "Stand up for what's right. Be an individual. Don't go with the crowd if that's not what you believe. Be prepared to be different." Powerful words to middle school students for whom belonging is so incredibly important.

After the speaker left, I asked my students what his words had meant to them. Forget politics, I said. Forget standing up against genocide in Bosnia or hatred in the Middle East. Tell me about being an individual in your own daily life. If someone makes an ethnic joke does anyone speak up? If a friend makes fun of a kid who's clearly an outsider, do you say anything? If everyone likes a certain band and you think it's awful, do you pretend to like it? To what lengths do you go to belong? I had no idea what the answers would be. On the one hand, I suspected that many would go to great lengths to fit in. But it also seemed to me that many of my students were strong individuals.

I devised an informal survey to allow my students the chance to respond anonymously, knowing full well that the results would be far from scientific.

I first asked, "How important is it for you to belong, fit in, not be different?" Eleven percent felt it was very important. Fifty percent felt it was sort of important, but they weren't going to do things they obviously knew were wrong in order to fit in. Thirty-nine percent felt it was not all that important. They just went along and tried to be themselves, or they prided themselves on being different.

On another part of the survey I asked, "If someone in your class who is really different were being picked on a lot by some of your friends, how would you react?

- Twenty-eight percent chose this answer: "I'd tell my friends to stop it. I can't stand that kind of thing. I feel secure enough that I know my friends aren't going to get mad at me for saying that. Plus, I think they'd listen to me."
- Twenty-six percent chose: "I'd tell my friends to stop it, but I'm not sure they'd listen, and I'm not sure they wouldn't get mad. I'd take the chance anyway."
- Nineteen percent chose: "I'd consider telling my friends to stop. I'd really want to tell them, but I might not."
- Five percent chose: I wouldn't like them torturing this kid, but I wouldn't dream of saying anything. I know they'd think I was weird for sticking up for him.
- Fourteen percent chose: I wouldn't say anything. It's the kid's own problem, not mine.
- Four percent chose: If the kid were really weird, I'd make fun of him, too.

The survey results were the starting point for a series of interesting discussions during which I began to wonder what young adult literature exists with the themes of standing up for others as well as for your true self, of daring to be different, of finding the courage to go against the tide. Here are some of the best books I found.

• The Cuckoo's Child

In *The Cuckoo's Child,* an award winning first novel by Suzanne Freeman, we meet Mia who longs to be "regular." She has grown up in a family of eccentrics who have lived for several years in Beirut, Lebanon. When her parents disappear during a cruise, she and her two older stepsisters are sent to live with their Aunt Kit in Tennessee while the authorities search for the missing parents.

The setting for Mia's coming of age is Vacation Bible School in the small town where Aunt Kit lives. Mia decides immediately that she wants to be part of the popular group. Instead, she ends up with what she labels "the losers" and becomes friends with Sinclair. Although Mia knows Sinclair is different and will never fit in, she likes her feisty personality and has fun with her.

But when Mia's chance to join the popular girls comes, she grabs it and dumps Sinclair on the spot. "I made the choice. I let her go," says Mia. Sinclair declares these other girls are "boring, snobby, and useless," but Mia is thrilled by the safety she feels with them. "Every day you know what to wear because Ellen or Cathy or one of them would call you to let you know." Freeman illuminates entire realms of adolescent culture with just a few words.

Mia hides her true self in order to fit in. When the girls ask what she likes to do, she considers telling them how much she loves poetry, how "when it was right, you felt it in some deep unknown part of yourself." Instead, she tells them she likes miniature golf. With this one incident, Freeman lets us feel what it's like to lie about what we truly love.

In the course of the story, Mia learns to accept herself. She realizes that she is not now and never will be "regular." She realizes the power she has when she is herself. "And I didn't need them after all. I could do what I wanted. I could dress how I wanted." It's a powerful realization.

She tries to make amends with Sinclair who, although willing to forgive her, is understandably wary. "How do I know you won't just go and join up with them again?" Sinclair asks.

Mia takes the question seriously. "The words terrified me. It was choosing the shape of your whole life. I said it. 'I can't go back. I tried it, and now I know. Sinclair, I just can't be regular.'" This is the theme that resonates so loudly in this magical first novel. Freeman has Mia tell her story with gentle humor and deep seriousness. By the end, I had come to love this cuckoo's child, who has accepted herself and begun to shape her own place in the world!

A small group of students who read this novel as part of a student-led book group found Freeman's style to be "excessively realistic." They were all accustomed to reading fantasy, and this foray into a different genre was not satisfying for them. As one student commented, "I am more of a fantasy buff, where the impossible happens and there is a sort of magical quality within the book. Realistic fiction is – well – a little too realistic for me. The book was boring and uneventful."

I wondered if Freeman's intense portrayal of a young girl's emotions made my students uncomfortable, especially when they had to talk about it in a group? Maybe it was easier to "bash the book" than to talk about feelings. Or was the book simply one of those that adults love but kids find boring? Do any middle school readers raised on the frantic pace of television and video games enjoy more slowly paced novels that focus on the inner life of a character?

I found three students who read *The Cuckoo's Child* independently and liked it. Alessandra, an eighth grader, said she really liked it, but "it is definitely not for people who don't like realistic fiction. The book had an interesting plot, but went slowly and was usually subdued, much like real life." She reads a lot of realistic fiction and felt that this one seemed "more like real life" than many."

To my surprise, Raghav, an active, sports-minded eighth grader, also enjoyed it. He found it "different" and enjoyed how Mia had kept changing her mind all the time. I think he was intrigued by this close up look at the working of another adolescent mind. He said it had "a little touch of mystery but also dealt with big issues."

My exploration of students' feelings about *The Cuckoo's Child* reminded me of something I had learned long ago but had been in danger of forgetting. It is absolutely impossible to predict what young adult readers will like! Yes, I can occasionally, maybe even fairly often if I'm knowledgeable and lucky, make a "hit" and recommend a book that an individual student will love. And I might even be lucky enough to choose one a group will like. But I have to be very careful not to fool myself into thinking that I have the inside track to their reading tastes!

TEACHING IDEA

Mia was lucky that Sinclair was such a forgiving friend. A story where the character is not so lucky is "Sucker" by Carson McCullers found in the anthology *Who Do You Think You Are? Stories of Friends and Enemies* selected by Hazel Rochman and Darlene Z. McCampbell.

"Sucker" shows the inhumanity of which we are all capable. Frustrated by his failed romance with the most beautiful girl in his class, Pete, the narrator, lashes out at his vulnerable young cousin, Sucker. But there is no redemption in this story, no forgiveness. Sucker becomes cold and distant and Pete is left alone with the consequences of his angry outburst. This would make a good read aloud and would provoke an interesting discussion among students who'd read *The Cuckoo's Child*.

• Daring To Be Abigail

The 11-year-old heroine of Rachel Vail's *Daring to Be Abigail* wrestles with the same issue as Mia. At summer Camp Nashaquitsa there are groups of insiders and outsiders. Abigail is determined to "reinvent" herself in order to fit in with the popular girls. It is clear to Abigail that who she is now is not adequate for membership in the popular group. So she tells her bunkmates that she never says no to a dare. In this "reinvention" of herself, she buries her kind and compassionate feelings for fellow camper, Dana, whom no one likes.

Vail reveals the insecurities of all the girls and shows how each, except for Dana, covers up her fears of being left out by always being on guard, watchful to do the "right" thing. Although Dana has some admittedly annoying traits, she is the first person who has ever bothered to ask about Abigail's father who died several years ago. This means a lot to Abigail, but when Tiffany, one of the most popular, self-assured girls, dares her to urinate in Dana's mouthwash, Abigail takes the dare.

When Abigail is kicked out of camp, she admits to her mother, "I like her. The girl I did this to. Dana. She knows how to be a friend. She was actually my best friend here." Unlike Mia, Abigail doesn't get a second chance at friendship with Dana. But she has learned a powerful lesson from the experience. At the close of the book she writes a letter to her dead father: "I'm not scared of the dark anymore, daddy, but now I'm scared of other things that a nightlight doesn't help because they are *in* me."

This is an easy book for younger middle school readers, but the message is a big one. As one of my mature, seventh grade readers wrote, "This is a short, entertaining, fun book to read. On the other hand you can go further into this book and really think about the concept behind it. Although it is a simple trip to summer camp, the choices she makes could change her forever." Indeed, Vail leaves the reader with the feeling that the biggest dare of all is to be yourself and to be true to your own feelings even if that leaves you on the outside.

TEACHING IDEA

Ask students to create their own survey where they try to find out how important it is for students to be popular and how far they would be willing to go to attain that popularity. You'll need to work

• Slot Machine
• Extreme Elvin

In *Slot Machine* by Chris Lynch, Elvin and his two best friends go to a summer retreat that is mainly an athletic camp. Elvin is overweight and clumsy and has no desire to be an athlete but is forced to go by his mother. Everyone at this camp is supposed to find his athletic slot. Elvin tries football. He tries baseball. Each is a disaster. Next, in wrestling, he thinks maybe he's found his niche. He likes wrestling. He even gets a book and studies it. But his progress is too slow, and they kick him out of the group.

Elvin describes a beer party in the woods that he, Mike, and Frankie attend. "Mike and I sat on a fallen tree and watched and listened, trying to somehow get it, to figure out what it was that was supposed to be so cool. I sipped my beer a few times, which I figured would help. It didn't, so I followed Mike's lead by pouring it out gradually so it looked like we were drinking it." While their friend Frankie is so desperate to belong that he is willing to humiliate himself and to take any kind of abuse the older guys dish out, Elvin and Mike remain true to their own sense of what is right.

In the end, Elvin ends up as a watcher. He decides that he wants to "watch people and think." He watches the arts and crafts group and hangs out with the other outsiders, the ones who are not jocks. He finds that he fits here even though he doesn't want to do any projects. He's comfortable with these other outsiders. As he tells Mike, "I don't know what my slot is, or what it's going to be, or if I'm ever going to find a slot. But I figure I could hang out with these guys while I'm waiting." Elvin leaves camp more confident that he is capable of finding his own way and doesn't need to fit into any of the camp's prescribed slots in order to be of value. He can be himself. I like this unpredictable, more realistic ending almost as much as I like Lynch's clear message that it's okay to be outside of society's slots. Lynch writes of the further adventures of Elvin in his sequel, *Extreme Elvin,* where he takes a humorous look at Elvin's freshman year in high school.

Students need to be encouraged to go beyond thinking about the plot of the book. One way to help them become more analytical is to have them write an essay describing the personality of one of the characters. I ask students to write about at least three character traits and to have at least three examples of things the character did that supports each trait.

It was difficult for some students to infer a character's personality from his actions, and this led to many informal conversations among students as they shared their insights about the characters. By talking and writing, students gradually become more aware of the character development in novels. Such a focus also helps middle grade students who are in the process of developing their own sense of self to see themselves and others more clearly. The assignment has proved to be good writing practice and has also encouraged students to think more deeply about books and themselves.

• CRASH

In any social setting, there are the outsiders, and then there are the self-appointed insiders who try to prevent the outsider from joining up. They have the same insecurities and fears that outsiders have, but somehow they've learned to cover up their shaky insides with a tough outer shell of bravado and, sometimes, downright meanness. In *CRASH*, Jerry Spinelli tells the story from the perspective of insider, John Coogan, a tough-talking jock who judges others by the price of their possessions and their skill at sports.

Spinelli makes no bones about revealing the shallowness of John, a.k.a. Crash, and his best friend, Mike. In sharp contrast to Crash and Mike is Penn Webb, a perky, vegetarian Quaker who lives down the street and has the courage of his convictions. Crash and Mike pick on him and play practical jokes. Penn takes it all without ever fighting back. Crash says Webb "doesn't know cool from fool."

Just when Crash is becoming so obnoxious that you wonder what you're doing reading this book, things begin to change. Scooter, Crash's much-loved grandfather has a stroke, and Crash gets a quick lesson in what really matters in life. Although he can't articulate it, he begins to realize that people, relationships, and love are what really count. He says of himself, "Crash Coogan. The Crash Man. Suddenly the name didn't seem to fit exactly. I had always thought my name and me were the same thing. Now there was a crack of daylight between them, like my shell was coming loose. It was scary." Crash Coogan is smack up against the conflict between the security of the self he knows and the dark abyss of his own unknown inner self.

In a selfless act of caring, Penn, despite the torture Crash has inflicted on him, brings a gift of great value to Scooter. Crash is so affected by this, that when Mike thinks up new and worse ways to torture Penn, Crash refuses to participate. In the end, Crash has grown enough to offer his own selfless gift to Penn. He ends the book by saying, "Penn Webb is my best friend." Hard to believe? One of my students said this transformation was a little unrealistic, but he liked the book anyway. I agree. Spinelli spins a cool tale, and I think we all want to believe that people can change. We want to believe that the tormenters can sometimes decide that the cost is too high and, like Crash, they can take a stand for the outsiders.

• Wringer

In another of Jerry Spinelli's novels, *Wringer,* the young hero must learn to stand up for himself. Palmer LaRue is probably the only boy in Waymer who doesn't want to be a wringer. At Waymer's annual Pigeon Day to raise money for the local park, hundreds of sharpshooters compete to shoot 5,000 pigeons. Young boys round up the dead and wring the necks of the wounded.

Palmer is a member of a small gang of boys, led by the despicable Beans, who delights in taunting others and for whom wringing the necks of pigeons is the highlight of the year. From the beginning, Palmer seems different to the reader, kinder, and more sensitive. But he denies this side of himself and is convinced that he loves being one of the gang. He accepts the nickname of Snots that Beans gives him and willingly abandons his old friend, Dorothy. Only when a pigeon lands outside his window and he takes it in and adopts it, hiding it in his room by night, letting it fly free by day, does he touch the softer part of his nature.

He keeps his pigeon, Nipper, a secret from everyone. When Beans suspects that he has a pigeon, he hotly denies it. "You're crazy! Why would I have a pigeon? I hate pigeons. I'm gonna be a wringer. I'm gonna wring their necks. I'm gonna whack 'em."

As the annual Pigeon Day draws closer, he dreads the time when he'll have to become a wringer. It's expected, not only by his friends but by a majority of the community. He believes that his father, too, expects it. To Palmer, becoming a wringer is the only way he can maintain his membership in the group, the only avenue to belonging.

Three quarters of the way through the book, Palmer begins to face up to facts. He "had come to realize that…the guys whose company he had once craved he now feared…He imagined them torturing him until he led them to his forbidden pet. At that point Nipper was as good as dead." Is he too weak, he wonders, to do anything other than to follow Beans?

As Pigeon Day approaches and Palmer's fears grow, the tension mounts. Finally, Palmer cracks. "He heard the scream, heard it coming a split second before the others heard it, the scream that he knew now had been growing inside him for a long time. He planted his feet and bent his knees and balled his fists and let it come all the way out: '…No wringer! No Snots!' He thrust his scream at Beans. 'I'm not Snots! My name is Palmer! My name is Palmer!' With this defiant act, Palmer shakes off the disguise he's been wearing for years and takes on his true identity – Palmer, a boy who is friends with Dorothy, a boy who loves a pigeon named Nipper, a compassionate boy who is not a member of a gang of tricksters and tormenters."

In a further act of bravery in front of the entire town gathered in the park for Pigeon Day, Palmer rescues Nipper from being shot. Spinelli seems to be saying it's not enough to declare yourself in front of your friends, you need to stand up for who you are in front of the community, too. Beyond the somewhat zany story line is the author's important message that although standing up for what you believe against the bullies of the world is never easy, it's the only way to find peace.

This was the only book that Nick, a bright sixth grader, loved all year. Every time he'd finish a book I'd say expectantly, "How'd you like it?" And every time he'd reply, "It was okay." "It didn't really grab you?" I'd ask, and he'd shake his head rather sadly. It became a joke between us, but I worried about his lukewarm attitude toward reading and wondered if he'd ever find a book he really liked. Then I recommended *Wringer* to him. Later, when I asked how he liked it, his eyes sparkled. "It was GREAT!" he said enthusiastically. At parent conferences, his mother told me that he'd talked a lot about it at home. "It's very unusual for Nick to talk about a book he's read." Ah, the magic of connecting the right student with the right book!

• Star Girl

Jerry Spinelli seems to be especially intrigued by the idea of peer pressure and insiders and outsiders. In *Star Girl,* a book for older middle grade readers, he takes yet another look at the issue, and this time he shows even more of its complexity.

Star Girl arrives at Mica High dressed in a long ruffled dress at least one hundred years out of style. She stands up in the middle of the lunchroom and serenades the student body as she strums her ukulele. In a high school that is "not exactly a hotbed of nonconformity," Star Girl stands out as **very** different. Spinelli paints her in bold, almost legend-like strokes.

She spreads a cloth over her desk in every class and puts flowers on it. She carries a mouse in her huge canvas bag. She leaves congratulatory cards for those who have performed a small kindness or received an "A" on a test. Students try to define her but can't get past words like goofy and weird. Leo observes that "In our minds we tried to pin her to a corkboard like a butterfly, but they merely went through and away she flew."

Soon, students get used to her boundless energy and crazy antics and look forward to seeing what she'll do next. She becomes a cheerleader and people decide they like having her around. But no one gets too close. "Because she was different. *Different.* We had no one to compare her to, no one to measure her against. She was unknown territory. Unsafe. We were afraid to get too close."

It's not long before Star Girl becomes a school-wide celebrity. People crowd around her lunch table, call to her in the hallways. Spinelli shows, however, that although she is suddenly the center of attention, no one has yet become her friend. Until one day Leo Borlock falls head over heels in love with her. Leo is a quiet, thoughtful, brilliant observer of Life, who avoids the spotlight, With Star Girl he discovers joy in small things and instead of being a "smiler" he becomes a person who laughs out loud.

Leo has always been well liked by his peers, but when the student body suddenly turns against Star Girl, they shun both her and Leo, the "Star Boy" who is her boyfriend. Torn between his feelings for Star Girl and his desire to fit in, he consults his friend and mentor, Archie, who wisely sums up his problem. "Whose affection do you value more, hers or the others?" Leo wrestles with this question, the heart of his conflict.

As the shunning begins to affect him more and more, Leo decides to convince Star Girl to become more "normal." He uses logic, explains it all gently. "You can't just wake up in the morning and say you don't care what the rest of the world thinks…This group thing…it's very strong…in a group everybody acts pretty much the same, that's kind of how the group holds itself together…We live in a world of them, like it or not." Star Girl disappears for a day and reappears as Susan (her birth name), dressed in designer labels, without her mouse and her ukulele and her strange ways. She has transformed her exterior into a "typical, ordinary, everyday, run-of-the-mill teenager."

But the shunning continues. Star Girl is convinced that if she wins the state oratorical contest, the students will forget their hatred of her and turn out en masse to congratulate her. She wins. When she returns to town, two teachers and one student are there to welcome her home. At this point she gives up on being "popular" and "normal" and returns to her true self. This is also the point at which Leo must make his decision. This is one of the many actions on Leo's part that will make for a lively discussion among students. He decides to go with the crowd and desert Star Girl. She and her family disappear and as the book ends 15 years later, Leo is still hoping he will someday find her again.

I like the realism of the ending. I like the fact that Spinelli exaggerated Star Girl so that students could more easily think about Leo's choice. I want my students to be able to connect this story to their own lives. There may be no Star Girls in your school, but there are certainly individuals who don't fit the "run-of-the-mill" mold. I was talking to a student recently who said he'd decided not to be a "nerd" any longer, but to be cool. It was a conscious decision, and, interestingly, he knew he was still a "nerd" inside. Will he be able to stick with this decision? How will it affect his life? Is there a price to pay for not being true to yourself? These are all important questions for our students to ponder. I've contemplated setting up a discussion group among high school students who've wrestled with this question and my middle school students. I've thought of having my students interview adults about how they handled this dilemma when they were adolescents. Reading good young adult literature leads me to think about these things and, I hope, to lead my students to a deeper understanding of their own conflicts and decisions.

• Crazy Lady

In Jane Leslie Conly's *Crazy Lady,* Vernon must also choose the shape of his life. Like the characters I've already discussed, he must decide what type of person he really is. Vernon's mom has died, and his dad is trying to keep the family together. Vernon hangs out with his friends and follows their lead when they make fun of Maxine Flooter when she lurches down the street, ranting and raving, often in a drunken stupor with her retarded son, Ronald.

Vernon's life changes when he fails English and is in danger of staying back in seventh grade. He hates school because of his own learning disabilities, and to stay back would be a fate worse than death. He willingly undertakes tutoring by the eccentric Miss Annie, a retired teacher who happens to live next door to Maxine and Ronald. Vernon is embarrassed that he used to make fun of Miss Annie and assures her that he "didn't really know her then." Miss Annie says, "It takes an effort to become friends with somebody different." It takes courage as well as effort, and Vernon demonstrates both as he slowly gets to know Maxine and Ronald as well as Miss Annie. He begins to see them as human beings rather than as targets for torments.

Vernon does more than just decide to stand up to his friends and stop teasing Maxine and Ronald. He organizes a neighborhood fair to raise money to buy Ronald a pair of sneakers so that he can enter the Special Olympics. He amazes himself with his organization skills and his ability to mobilize the entire neighborhood.

In the end, Maxine must send Ronald to live with relatives in another state because she can no longer care for him. The book ends on a sad note as Vernon tries to cope with the loss of his friend. Conly has written a simple story that shows how one person, like Vernon, can make a difference to an individual, a family, a neighborhood. The moral is clear but not too heavy-handed for younger middle school students.

• Daphne's Book

Daphne's Book has always been one of my favorite Mary Downing Hahn's books. Like Vernon, Jessica becomes friends with an outsider. She is paired with Daphne, the outsider with the mismatched clothing who keeps to herself and is considered strange, for a school project. To her surprise, she discovers that she enjoys Daphne's company, and they become close friends.

Even though she likes Daphne, she is not quite ready to acknowledge the friendship in public and to face the taunting of the other girls. When she's at McDonald's with Daphne, and the other girls from school come in, she hides in the bathroom to avoid being seen with her. Another time, when Daphne's grandmother, Mrs. Woodleigh, who is mentally ill, causes a scene in the drugstore, Jessica fails to go to Daphne's aid. "Although I was ashamed of myself, I hid like a coward among the L'eggs eggs, my face burning. I wanted to help Daphne, but I couldn't force myself to walk past the people watching Mrs. Woodleigh's performance. I knew they would all look at me, waiting to see what new entertainment I was going to provide. I hated myself, but I didn't take a step toward Daphne. Not one."

Later, shamed by her lack of courage, she speaks up and tells the other girls to stop making fun of Daphne. They laugh and continue. Only her friend Tracy sees how upset she is, and together they leave the other girls. As one of my students wrote on the survey, "If they don't respect my position, then they aren't really my friends." Brave words. Hahn writes with sympathy of the very real difficulty of going against the tide, no matter how small the incident may seem to us as adults. This is a great book for younger middle grade students.

• Plague Year

In *Plague Year* by Stephanie S. Tolan, a book for older middle grade readers, she imagines what would happen to a serial killer's teenage son when the father is arrested and his story appears on the front page of every newspaper in the nation.

The first day Bran Slocum appears at Ridgewood High, no one knows his terrible secret. But they know right away that he's different. They judge him immediately by his appearance – ponytail, scarves, an earring, and a face that looked as if it had been "carved out of stone." He instantly becomes a target for the class bullies.

David, the narrator, runs track and tries to keep a low profile. His best friend is Molly who told him at the beginning of high school, "You do the regular high school stuff for both of us…If anything interesting happens you can tell me all about it. That way, I won't miss anything, but I won't have to figure out how to change myself into somebody I'm not just to fit in." And so it comes as no surprise when Molly befriends Bran and takes on the bullies. When the bullies physically attack Bran, Molly stands up to them. Later, she berates David for not helping her. "You let me go after those guys all by myself. You and every other person here. Doesn't anybody understand? It would only take a couple of guys *not* letting them get away with stuff like that, and they'd have to stop. God, what cowards people are!"

David's reply is the classic answer to such an accusation: "Molly, get real. Bruno is Bruno. Nobody's going to go up against him when he's by himself, let alone when he's surrounded by his goons. Nobody even wants to." Ask your students how they feel and what they do when they see a classmate being picked on. It's a situation students encounter all the time, and their response has probably become automatic. This book forces them to think about choices and consequences.

Once students and their parents discover that Bran's father is the serial killer who was arrested in another state, things get even worse. Some parents don't want their children going to school with Bran. They want him out of school and out of town. Others, like David's dad, want to stay uninvolved. He says to David, "There are rotten things in the world that you can't fix. No matter how much you hate them, you can't fix them. You and Molly are young enough that you still think you can, but you'll learn. You tell her to stay away from this kid. There's not a thing in the world she can do for him. And she doesn't want to get mixed up with whatever happens." We can see where David got his desire to remain uninvolved. But David is not his father. And to him, his father's words sound cowardly. Molly pushes him at every opportunity to get involved. When David repeats his father's sentiments by telling her "You can't change his life…" Molly shoots back with, "You said last night I was his friend. Well, I am. And don't tell me having a friend doesn't make a difference. It does. I know."

Gradually, David gets more and more involved. As he gets to know Bran, he finds himself liking him. David is sensitive and tries to understand how impossibly difficult it must be to discover your father has killed a number of young kids and buried them in the back yard. As the townspeople turn more and more ugly with fear and hatred, he makes a choice to be on Bran's side.

The story ends with a tragic confrontation late at night at the quarry and the death of Bran and two of the bullies. This might be too much for some younger middle school readers but for most seventh and eighth graders it's exactly the type of realistic fiction they need to read and discuss. David and Molly made a choice that night that leads to the death of one of the bullies. What would your students have chosen in such a situation?

Molly has called the events that began with Bran's arrival in town and ended with his death at the quarry, "the plague." But David decides that "plague" is the wrong term. "This wasn't something that came from outside. It was inside all of us, whatever it was. And it still is." What can you do when you discover this rather horrifying truth about yourself? The book ends with Tolan's answer. In the last paragraph, David makes a firm decision to go to college and "do something" with his life, "…something to stand against what I found inside myself that night. I don't know what I'll do, yet. I just know it will be something that makes a difference." Most of our students are still idealistic. Knowing that they *can* make a difference is one of the most important things they can learn in middle school.

TEACHING IDEA

An excellent short story that shows the difficulties of going against the tide is, "Celia Behind Me" by Isabel Huggan in the anthology *Who Do You Think You Are? Stories of Friends and Enemies* selected by Hazel Rochman and Darlene Z. McCampbell.

"Celia Behind Me" is the story of an outsider, an overweight, diabetic child who is picked on by others. Elizabeth, the narrator, who is worried about her own place in the group, turns on Celia in a violent verbal and physical attack that leaves her stunned at the darkness in her own nature.

This story makes a great read-aloud or you could have students discuss it in small groups.

• Drummers of Jericho

In Carolyn Meyer's *Drummers of Jericho,* Pazit Trujillo is an outsider in the small, tightly knit, largely Christian community of Jericho where she's moved to live with her father and stepmother. Everything about her is different – her city attitudes, her Jewish heritage, and the clothes she wears. Insider Billy Harper, who has lived in Jericho all his life, meets her during the summer and finds her fascinating. When school starts he pretends not to know her because he knows his friends think she's strange.

When the school band starts to practice for a state competition and are playing Christian hymns and marching in the formation of a cross, Pazit refuses to march. The ACLU gets involved and the tension in Jericho rises. Meyer tells clearly how alone and frightened Pazit feels as she is subjected to name calling, threats against her dog, and other forms of hostility.

Of Billy, Meyer says, "He had been pretty much like everybody else. He had always tried to fit in. Everyone he knew had grown up the same way he had, believing in the same kind of things. He had never questioned any of that…until he met Pazit." Now Billy finds himself at a school board meeting attended by most of the town and everyone is speaking in favor of continuing the band's marching plans. Billy's mother forces him to get up and speak. "Just talk about how you feel," she tells him. Billy stands up, not quite sure what words will come out of his mouth. To the amazement of his friends, family and, most of all himself, the words are in defense of Pazit.

"The easy thing, his dad had always told him is to go along with the crowd. The hard thing is to stand alone and do what's right." Billy finds out how hard it is to stand alone when his friends stop speaking to him and his girlfriend breaks up with him.

I like the way this eighth grade student describes Billy: "In the beginning when Billy was avoiding Pazit in school I thought he was one of those kids who blend in, but he changed and became very independent, going back to listening to his own heart."

The characters are appealing and multi-dimensional. Pazit has problems with her mother and is annoyed with her father when he calls in the ACLU. Billy hesitates and stumbles before taking each step. His dilemma and eventual courageous stand are drawn with sympathy and realism. One of the major weaknesses is that we never get a sense of what motivates Billy. Where did he get his sense of fairness and his lack of prejudice?

Although the school is forced to change its band music and marching plans, the rest of the story is left unresolved. Of one thing we can be certain. Billy Harper will never be the same. His encounter with Pazit, his courage in standing up to an entire town, has surely shaped the rest of his life.

• Music From a Place Called Half Moon

Music from a Place called Half Moon by Jerrie Oughton is the moving story of Edie Jo Houp who, like Billy, challenges the narrow-minded bigotry of a small town even though she does it in a quieter, far less public way than Billy. Half Moon, North Carolina, in 1956 was a town where people were afraid of differences.

Edie Jo's father takes the first step toward breaking the barriers between Whites and Indians when he speaks out in favor of letting the local Indian children attend Vacation Bible School. Edie Jo, as well as most of the townspeople are horrified. Edie Jo says, "I could take an Indian or two at one time…But having them to your house? Drinking out of your glasses and sitting at your table? I was pretty sure I wasn't ready for that. Might never be."

An eighth grade girl liked the plot of this book because of the fact "that the prejudice was not against African Americans like it usually is in books set in the 1950s. It's not very often that you find a book that focuses on prejudice toward a different minority group."

When Edie Jo and her older brother experience a frightening incident in which they are threatened by a group of Indians, Edie Jo's feelings intensify. "I hated people of color. All of them. I was afraid of them, and I hated them."

Getting to know one individual changes Edie Jo's feelings. She meets Cherokee Fish, and they cautiously develop a close friendship. As he shares his harmonica music and she her deeply felt poetry, they learn to trust each other and discover they are not so different after all.

Edie Jo and Cherokee Fish develop their friendship in complete privacy at a secret refuge at a sawmill. It is only when Cherokee is killed in a shocking act of violence that their friendship is made public.

Valerie, another eighth grader who read this book, noted, "I never got to know Cherokee well enough before he died, and I felt extremely unsatisfied. If I'd known more it would have been upsetting when he died, but I'm sure I'd have found it more fulfilling."

As Edie Jo struggles to cope with her grief, she overhears her father say to her mother, "I wish there would come about a change in Half Moon. In the world. Where people wouldn't crush each other with their prejudices. I wish there were just one thing I could find to do to begin that." She, too, wants to do something to make a difference. So she takes a chance and reaches out in friendship to Cherokee Fish's younger sister, Leona. "Finally I knew where I stood. One at a time, I could accept people for who they were. Leona could come to my house. She could come drink out of my glasses and sit at my table because she was a person. A human being I had learned to value."

One of the strengths of this book is Oughton's portrayal of how Edie Jo changes. In a character essay about Edie Jo, Alessandra talks about her thoughtfulness and gives several examples of it. Then she says,

"There's one thing I must point out about this trait though. As soon as Edie Jo does something thoughtless she realizes she was wrong. Sometimes right away and other times it takes her a while to figure out exactly where she went wrong…She becomes less and less thoughtless as the book goes on and she realizes how to open up and feel for others, not just herself. A good example of this is after Cherokee died. The night he died Edie Jo had taken his harmonica from his pocket. About a week later Edie Jo gave Cherokee's sister, Leona, the harmonica. This was a very kind and thoughtful thing to do. Edie could have just kept it to herself and used it as a reminder of her friend. But, instead, she thought about how his family must have felt and decided to give them something that mattered very much to Cherokee. This is truly a selfless act. I think Edie Jo had done a lot of growing during that summer because of all that had happened."

It is important for students to think about the ways that characters change during a novel. I often remind them that if they can figure out how the main character has changed they'll probably have a clue to the theme of the book. Alessandra and I had several conversations as she was writing her essay, and I encouraged her to look for changes and to incorporate them into her essay. I explained that showing the complexity of a character and how her traits change over the course of the book makes for a more sophisticated essay.

• Spite Fences

Maggie Pugh is yet another character who chooses to stand up to an entire town. Trudy Krisher, the author of *Spite Fences*, raises the questions: What does it take to stand up to a bully who sexually threatens you? How much courage do you need to stand up to an entire town full of bigotry and hate? Does a 13-year-old girl, a girl who seems so ordinary on the outside, a girl like many of your students and mine, have this much courage?

It is the summer of 1960 and Maggie Pugh lives in Kinship, Georgia, a town divided by race and class. Maggie is White, and her family is poor. Her father is out of work, her mother is dangerously close to being out of hope, and Maggie is helping to hold the family together with the ten dollars she gets each month for cleaning.

There are rules in Kinship, unwritten, unspoken rules that have to do with how members of the Black community are treated. Blacks have their own school, church, and park. At Byer's Drugs, they have separate bathrooms and are not allowed to sit at the counter. As the book opens, Maggie has already broken one of these rules by being friends with Zeke, a Black peddler. No one knows how much she admires Zeke's strength or that she's secretly teaching him to read.

Maggie has other secrets, too. First there's the secret that the man whose house she cleans is a Black professor who has come to town to help Black people win their rights. There's also the way her mother treats her. Mama's last remaining hopes rest on Maggie's younger sister, Gardenia, winning the Little Miss Contest. Mama dotes on Gardenia. With Maggie she's harsh and critical. Coupled with the beatings she gives her (one with a thorned rose stem) it would be called child abuse today.

But the hardest secret of all for Maggie to keep is what she witnessed last summer from her perch in a tree at the Negro park. A group of white men attacked her friend Zeke so brutally that she's been unable to tell anyone. I would warn students that the book contains several graphic scenes of violence and while they are completely appropriate for the book's setting, they may be disturbing to younger middle grade readers.

The story unfolds slowly. After Maggie is threatened by her 17-year-old neighbor, Virgil Boggs, who was one of the young men who attacked Zeke, Maggie's mother decides to build a high fence around their house.

Unlike most of the people around her, Maggie is open-minded and she learns a lot from her friend Zeke and from George Hardy, the professor whose house she cleans. Mr. Hardy gives her a look at the bigger world outside Kinship. Both men teach her the perils of fear and spite and building fences. As Maggie's world expands, she is called upon to help fight the bigotry and fear in Kinship. She is up against a town full of bullies, but in her heart, she knows what is right.

With amazing courage she begins by refusing to live any longer with her mother's abuse and leaves home to live with her friend Pert Wilson. (See Chapter 2 for the review of *Kinship*, Pert's own story of life in Kinship.) Then Maggie takes on the entire town by agreeing to testify in court what she saw the men do to Zeke last summer.

Throughout the book, Maggie is interested in photography as a way of seeing and telling the truth. When her Black friends decide to stage a peaceful sit-in at Byer's lunch counter, Maggie is there with her camera. When the sit-in turns violent, she captures it all on film and sells the photos to *Life* magazine. This is Maggie's way of standing up to the injustice in Kinship and in the entire South.

Each of these acts of bravery by a young girl can inspire our students to take a stand against bullies and injustice in their worlds.

TEACHING IDEA

Many of the books in this chapter could be integrated well into a study of equality and justice in America. *Us and Them: A History of Intolerance in America* is an exceptionally well-written book by Jim Carnes. It describes American history from a Quaker woman in 1660 who risked her life for religious freedom to a 1991 conflict among ethnic groups in Brooklyn, New York. There are chapters on racial hatred against Chinese laborers in the late 1800s, Japanese Americans during World War II, African Americans in the '20s and '80s and many more.

The **Teaching for Tolerance** project also has an excellent video that accompanies the book. For information contact: Teaching Tolerance, 400 Washington Ave., Montgomery, AL 36104 or phone (344) 264-0286. The web site for this organization is at http://www.Tolerance.org/.

• Twelve Days in August
• Blue Coyote

Another book that makes for great discussions and that was very popular with many of my students is *Twelve Days in August* by Liza Ketchum Murrow, who is now writing under the name Liza Ketchum. At first glance, it reads like a sports story, but it is so much more than that. Todd, co-captain of the soccer team, lives for soccer. When Alex, an exceptional athlete and a newcomer to the small Vermont town, joins the team, Todd thinks they finally have a chance for a winning season. But the team quickly becomes dysfunctional when Randy starts spreading rumors that Alex is gay. Randy and his friends are determined to get Alex off the team. Although Todd has become friends with Alex, he tries desperately to stay uninvolved, afraid to defend Alex for fear of being similarly labeled.

Ketchum has a light and appropriate touch on this controversial subject. Of the growing number of novels available on this important issue, this is the one you would probably feel most comfortable discussing with students. The reader never learns for sure if Alex is gay although there are numerous clues that he is. (In the sequel, *Blue Coyote*, Alex has moved to Los Angeles and learns to deal with his sexuality. Many of the students who enjoyed this book were eager to read *Blue Coyote*. Those who did reported that it was even better than *Twelve Days in August*.)

Ketchum uses dialogue effectively to reveal character and advance the plot. The minor characters are well drawn, but Todd has center stage, and she shows us his thoughts and feelings as the tension mounts during these 12 days of soccer practice. She describes both the strategies and the spirit of the game, and readers who like soccer will appreciate the many soccer scenes. Todd's troubles with his girlfriend and his relationship with his family make the story equally interesting for non-sports fans. A student who is a soccer player said that in his opinion the author did a great job with the soccer scenes. He also enjoyed the way the author dealt with the big issues of relationships and loyalty.

But, in my mind, what really makes this book special is the theme that one individual has the power to make a choice and by his actions influence the group to also make the "right" choice. Todd finally finds the courage to get off the fence and come to Alex's defense and, in doing so, discovers he has a power he never dreamed of. Ketchum is never didactic, but the message is clear and the idea is a powerful one for adolescents to think about and discuss. Todd is a wonderful role model for adolescents who are debating whether to take the risk of going against the crowd. I believe one of the reasons this novel was so popular with my students is because Ketchum writes so knowingly about the pressures adolescents feel to be part of the group.

Young adolescents need role models, both real and fictional, who are not afraid to take the risk, to swim against the tide, to stand tall and speak out, to risk becoming an outsider, to be, above all, true to their real inner selves.

In *Music From a Place Called Half Moon,* Edie Jo's father sums up the theme of all the books in this chapter when he says, "...sometimes a person is given the opportunity to do something right, to stand for something. It don't happen every day. When that doorway opens, you gotta go through it or be forever looking back, wishing you had."

Drawing by Kyle Norris

Books stretch my imagination, and each time I finish one, I feel like I'm a new person. —Sarah Harmon, Grade 6

Chapter 2: A Tangle of Emotions
— Novels about family relations —

I don't usually read this kind of book," Chris said as I handed him a copy of Ouida Sebestyen's *Out of Nowhere.*

"I know," I said, smiling. I thought of the books he had been reading lately–a lot of Jay Bennett mysteries, some R.L. Stine, a few fantasies, but no realistic fiction. "I think it would be interesting for you to try something a little different. Your taste in reading can change and you won't know it has if you don't experiment now and then."

He took the book and agreed to give it a try. I wondered how he would like it. Two weeks later he wrote:

My first impression of *Out of Nowhere* was that it was slow. The beginning didn't grab me like a Jay Bennett book. I thought this was going to be a horrible book, but as I got into it, my views changed. I was actually eager to keep reading. This is the first lengthy book about families that I've read in my life, so it took a little getting used to. If you hadn't assigned this to me, I wouldn't have picked it up, but I'm glad I read it. I rate it a 10.

Like Chris, many of my students would not pick up a "family book" on their own. Why? "Too much of that emotional stuff," said one student. "Too slow. Not enough action," said another. While I give them a lot of freedom to read books of their own choice, I occasionally like to assign a book for a small group discussion that will stretch their reading experience. Even though it does not always end up with every student loving the assigned book, there can sometimes be a magical connection!

The best realistic fiction deals with that "emotional stuff." I want my students to read books that are rich with the portrayal of strong, well-developed characters who are struggling with the same tangle of emotions and conflicts they encounter in their own lives. I want them to meet characters who examine their parents' values and choices and try to determine how to live their own lives. For your consideration here is some of the best realistic fiction about families.

• Plain City

As adolescents evaluate their parents' lives and begin to see them as individuals, they are bound to find mistakes they have made. No one is perfect (least of all one's own parents). *Plain City,* by Virginia Hamilton is about mistakes and forgiveness. Twelve-year-old Buhlaire Sims is a bold, straight-talking heroine of mixed racial background who is trying to find her place in the world. She lives with her mother, a singer and dancer who is often away, two aunts, and an uncle. She has always believed her father died in Vietnam, but one day she accidentally discovers that he is alive and living nearby.

In a memorable scene, Buhlaire braves a blizzard and finds him living with other homeless people in an underpass. He wants her to bring him money so they can go away together. She struggles with a turmoil of feelings – her anger at the rest of her family for concealing the truth and her love for her father and desire to help him. At the same time there is a growing realization that his mind is not quite right.

Grady, a boy from school, and Buhlaire develop a close friendship. Grady's dad runs the homeless shelter in town and he provides an interesting contrast to Buhlaire's dad who is unable to pull his life together. He helps Buhlaire forgive her family and make the right decision about whether to go with her dad. "The hardest thing is understanding that our parents aren't perfectly good," he says, "...they make mistakes. They're human."

As Buhlaire works with her uncle to help flood victims she realizes that with acceptance and forgiveness of her family comes a change in her whole outlook on life. "It's exciting, life is," she says to herself. Hamilton sensitively describes the relationships and the tough decisions Buhlaire is trying to sort out.

One of my students who rated this book very highly wrote,

"To me this book seemed so real, like it could be a real kid that this is happening to. In the beginning, Buhlaire seemed mean and tough, but I think she was mad and hurt that her mom had lied to her about her dad. It was a wonderful book. I liked it from the beginning and then it just got better and better."

• From the Notebooks of Melanin Sun

In all families, the parents make choices that directly affect the lives of the children. Sometimes the child has a difficult time accepting these choices. Jacqueline Woodson's *From the Notebooks of Melanin Sun* deals with this theme. Melanin, a young African American, is a quiet, sensitive boy, who lives with his mother. Woodson skillfully shows the close, loving relationship they have. One day, Mama wants him to meet someone special. He assumes it is a new boyfriend but it turns out to be Kristen, a white woman Mama met in a law class.

In an emotional scene, Mama confides that she is in love with Kristen. Mel is overwhelmed by this information, drowning in his own fear. He shuts himself up in his room, shuts Mama out and pours all his feelings into his notebook. Does this make *him* gay? What will his friends say? And what does it mean for the future of his relationship with Mama? Mel wrestles with his emotions in a clear and honest voice.

Readers will be able to relate to his uncertainty, about his being different, his shyness with girls, and his sadness when one of his friends taunts him about his mother. Another friend sticks by him, however, and says, "It's no big deal, you know. Like what goes on with your mother doesn't have to do with anybody else, right?" This is what Mel slowly comes to accept. He finally agrees to give Kristen a chance and finds himself liking her. She's a lot like his mother and they share a deep love of nature.

Woodson is realistic. She shows us that Mel knows the future is uncertain and it probably will not be easy. But he also knows that he and Mama will always love each other, and, as he says, "…for the quickest moment ... I was sure of me." Building confidence step by painfully slow step and getting ready to leave the family, and build a life of your own, are a big part of what adolescence is all about.

From the Notebooks of Melanin Sun is an easy read but one that is definitely filled with "that emotional stuff." Because Woodson gets the emotional scenes right, a number of my students rated this book highly.

• Belle Prater's Boy

All parents make mistakes, some more terrible than others. Sometimes their choices leave painful wounds and deep scars. *Belle Prater's Boy* by Ruth White is about being strong enough to face up to the hurt caused by parents and to forgive them. In the end, it's what we all must do.

It's also a story about secrets. One morning Belle Prater disappears. Her son, Woodrow, comes to live with his grandparents, and soon he and his cousin, Gypsy, who lives next door, become close friends. The mystery of Belle's disappearance hangs over the entire story. There's gentle humor here and both sadness and joy as the children go about their everyday lives.

In an unexpected twist, we discover that Woodrow is not the only one with a secret hanging over his life. Gypsy's father died when she was five and she believes it was as a hero in a fire. Everyone else knows he shot himself in the face, and Gypsy was the one who discovered the body. When a mean schoolmate blurts out the true story, Gypsy enraged at her dead father, chops off all her hair, hair that he had always admired and praised. "I am not your Beauty now," she sneers. Her mother reassures her that in time she'll get over being angry at him for choosing to leave them.

Woodrow, too, must forgive the mother who abandoned him. Although we never learn for sure what happened to her, Woodrow believes she left with a traveling carnival. What hurts more than her leaving is that she never tried to contact him. He's read all the personal ads that they used to read together, hoping she'd choose to get in touch. "She still might do it, Woodrow," Gypsy says encouragingly. Woodrow replies, "No, she won't. She's gone. She won't ever look back now. I've known it for a long time, but it don't hurt as much as it used to." Gypsy realizes, "It was a moment, I reckon, when we both faced the truth. Aunt Belle had left Woodrow on purpose just like my daddy left me. Not because they didn't love us. They did. But their pain was bigger than their love. You had to forgive them for that." It's a satisfying conclusion to a complicated situation, but perhaps it's just a bit too neatly wrapped up and the children just a bit too wise and accepting for their age.

• Zel

In *Zel,* Donna Jo Napoli (see her book *Stones in Water* in Chapter 3) also writes about forgiveness of a parent. She takes the Grimm fairy tale, *Rapunzel,* and re-tells it in a Medieval setting in Switzerland in the mid-1500s. Students who are interested in writing styles will be intrigued by Napoli's technique of alternating chapters among Zel, a delightful young girl just reaching puberty, Mother, a woman who tricked her neighbors into giving her baby Zel, and Konrad, the spoiled son of a count who falls in love with Zel. Students might wish to speculate on why the chapters that focus on Zel and Konrad are written in third person while Mother's story is in first person.

But *Zel* is much more than a study in writing techniques. Although it has the feeling of a fairy tale complete with characters with magical powers, it is also a modern psychological study of the tangled emotions that exist between mother and daughter. It would be very interesting to do a mother and daughter reading group with this book!

Mother and Zel live in an isolated alm and only go to town twice each year. They have a loving and close relationship, but Zel is turning 13, and she loves the trips to town and the chance to be with other people. She is, like all thirteen-year-olds, beginning to grow away from her mother.

When Mother goes to buy cloth to make a birthday dress for Zel, the cloth merchant's wife suggests that if Zel is 13 she will probably be married within the year. Mother is horrified by this idea and thinks to herself, "Zel will not be wed within the year. No. She must not leave me. This dress-to-be is perfect. Why has the clerk tainted my gift with her mundane talk of marriage? I am filled with elation at the thought of Zel's beauty in this dress and dread at the thought that anyone other than me should appreciate that beauty. The contradictory emotions merge hatefully,… so that I cannot pick them apart." Tangled emotions indeed!

Mother works hard to keep her "arms from becoming iron…As much as I would want to, I must not shackle Zel to me. I love her. That love must be returned freely. I cannot bear anything less." But when her attempts to persuade Zel to promise to give up marriage in return for a gift of talking to animals fail, Mother cannot resist the temptation to use her magic to do exactly what she has sworn to herself not to do.

Mother discovers that Zel is constantly thinking about Konrad, the young count she met at the market, and she decides she must take no more risks. She locks Zel away in a deserted tower deep in the woods. With her magical powers she makes Zel's hair grow rapidly so she can ascend and descend from the tower each day to visit.

We can only imagine the desperation Zel feels at being locked away from everything she loves in life. Mother has convinced Zel that there is an enemy searching for her who would kill her if he found her. As her desperation grows, Zel begs Mother to take her home.

"Someday you will tire of looking for this enemy. You seem near exhaustion when you come."

"I will never tire of it, Zel. I will protect you forever."

The words chill Zel more than the fall winds, more than anything else Mother could have said.

And Zel gives up hope of escaping and becomes filled with despair.

In the meantime, Konrad is obsessed with Zel and only finds her after two years of desperately searching for her. But he rescues her only to lose both her and his vision due to Mother's magic. Zel escapes and for another two years, raises her twin daughters and comes to terms with her feelings about her mother. She remembers the 13 good years they had together. "Mother was a good mother. The alm was a good place to stretch and grow…Mother was a witch…[Zel] has read and reread the faces of the people of her town. They are good faces, kind faces. She looks into these faces and she believes there isn't a one of them who wouldn't sell his soul for the right price. She has to believe this. She loved Mother." As she raises her daughters with tenderness "her heart opens" and she accepts that she "owes her soul to the witch woman." As we would say in modern psychological terms, Mother was doing the best she could and by accepting it, the daughter is able to get on with her own life.

Like all good fairy tales, this one has a happy ending. Konrad finds Zel and his baby daughters, her tears cure his blindness and they all live happily ever after. And depending on how you interpret the last sentence, it's possible that Mother lives happily too. The last sentence reads, "And they [Zel and Konrad] see each other and, yes, oh, yes, we are happy." Throughout the book, only Mother's thoughts have been written in the first person. An alternate interpretation would be that Zel has now become free and she has taken over the first person narration. Students will have a good time debating which ending they think Napoli intended. Personally, I'd like to believe the fairy tale ended happily for everyone, even Mother.

• One Bird

One Bird by Kyoko Mori is also about love and forgiveness. Set in Japan in 1975, it begins when 15-year-old Megumi's mother, unable to tolerate her husband's unfaithfulness any longer, leaves Megumi and her father. He orders them to have no contact as long as Megumi is living in his home. Although her mother agrees to write secretly to her, she refuses to call her or see her. Megumi is filled with anger and fear. It will be seven years before she is through school and will be able to see her mother again. How could her mother leave her behind with her cold, distant father and critical grandmother?

The story traces Megumi's growth toward independence. As she tells of her day-to-day activities and reflects on her childhood memories, we come to know the two important women in her life. First, there is her mother, who has tried to fit herself into the mold of perfect Japanese woman. Then there is Megumi's new friend, the single, self-reliant veterinarian who teaches her not only to care for injured birds but to be her own person. Unlike Megumi's mother, she does not conform to Japanese society's stereotype of what a woman should he like. Megumi examines these two role models as she seeks to define her own identity and to come to terms with her mother's betrayal.

Megumi is a bright and complex young woman. She speaks clearly of her pain – the loss of childhood friends who have changed as they have grown up; the coldness of her father and grandmother; the unrequited love of a young man; and, most of all, the loss of her mother. She acknowledges her own flaws and mistakes with a refreshing honesty. When she finally decides to stand up to her father and demand the right to visit her mother, the reader wants to jump up and cheer. Megumi is well on her way to becoming a strong woman who can make her own choices and assert her rights despite the rules of her father or of society. Both adolescents and adults will be able to relate to the complex web of feelings she seeks to unravel.

There is much to discuss about this complex book, and I remember several years ago having a series of lively conversations with a group of girls who had read it. It proved a little too difficult for even excellent sixth graders so I'd recommend it only for older readers. It's also a good book to read as part of a cultural study of Japan.

• Tangerine

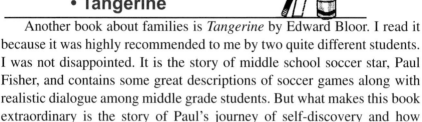

Another book about families is *Tangerine* by Edward Bloor. I read it because it was highly recommended to me by two quite different students. I was not disappointed. It is the story of middle school soccer star, Paul Fisher, and contains some great descriptions of soccer games along with realistic dialogue among middle grade students. But what makes this book extraordinary is the story of Paul's journey of self-discovery and how seamlessly it is woven into the unfolding of everyday life.

Paul has known for a long time that his father pays a great deal of attention to his older brother, Erik, and what Paul refers to as the "Erik Fisher Football Dream." Erik is a high school football star, and Mr. Fisher is determined he'll go on to the big time. By focusing his energies on Erik, he virtually ignores Paul's existence. Although his mother drives him to school and to soccer practice and talks to him, she seems distant and preoccupied with her own problems.

The deeper you get into the book, the more you begin to realize that Bloor is portraying a dysfunctional family set in the midst of a suburban life filled with empty and self-absorbed people. But Paul is different. He senses that he has different values than the people around him and when his school is swallowed by a huge sinkhole, he winds up in a neighboring school filled with tough kids from outside the suburbs. He enters not just a new school but an entirely new world. He struggles to be accepted by his new soccer team, especially by Tino and his sister Theresa whose family runs a citrus farm. When the temperature drops and the fruit is in danger, Paul pitches in to help. He especially admires Tino's older brother, Luis, who has invented a new variety of citrus called Golden Dawn.

Paul is shocked when Luis suddenly dies from a blow to the head. He knows who struck the blow, and he knows he must speak out regardless of the consequences. Paul says, "I thought about Luis Cruz, a man I barely knew. I thought about Luis Cruz being lowered into this ground, never to come back up. I felt the tears start to well up deep inside of me. Once they started to come, there was no stopping them. I wept, and sobbed, and poured tears into that hole in the ground. Like an idiot? No, I don't think so."

Like so many young adolescents, Paul is sorting out his own values and deciding where he stands and who he is. He finds, as perhaps many of our students do, that his own developing values are not the same as the rest of his family's. He cares about the people who live outside the suburbs. He cares about the citrus fruit and the people who grow it. He doesn't want to live in an insulated world that keeps him from knowing a variety of people. Most of all, Paul cares about the truth, and his family has not been telling him the truth for most of his life. Paul finds the courage to take a stand for what he knows is right and to strike off in his own direction, as, ultimately, each individual must do. In this book whose richness comes from its portrayal of both the everyday life of middle school students and the inner life of one sensitive and compassionate middle school boy, students can perhaps discover a little bit more about themselves. Every student who's read it so far has told me that it's a great book!

• Sons of Liberty

Sons of Liberty, a small but powerful book by Adele Griffin that was a 1997 National Book Award Finalist, has an important message for young readers that is similar to that of *Tangerine.* You can become like your parents and repeat their lives, or you can choose to be yourself and create your own life.

Rock has a complicated relationship with his father. Rock is not a perfect kid, but he's a normal guy who loves his dad. But his dad is not a perfect guy either. Far from it. His dad is into power and control. In the opening scene his dad wakes Rock and his older brother, Cliff, in the middle of the night to go fix a leak in the roof. This is what Rock calls an "interrupted night" and what his dad says builds character. His father is skillful at playing one son against the other. "Don't know how I got one son so alert and one so lazy," he says to Rock when Cliff is reluctant to get up. But at other times he yells at Rock for his stupidity and praises Cliff for being the bright one.

As the story unfolds, we learn more about the history of the family, of how they moved to Connecticut and could only afford to rent a summer cottage. But the lack of insulation and ensuing cold didn't bother the father. He said it built strength. He wanted his sons to grow up tough.

In one of the saddest scenes in the book, Rock recalls a time when he saved his money and bought lobsters for the family for a special event. His father berated him for spending too much and threw them into the fireplace ashes. Another example of his meanness is how he treats his young daughter. In addition to wounding her with his harsh indictment of her bedwetting, he takes away her favorite doll as a punishment.

Rock has a cruel streak of his own and is often in trouble for fighting at school. In one scene he and his friend Liza throw a snowball with a rock in it at a boy they dislike. We clearly see the possibility of Rock growing up to be like his father.

Rock is the obedient son, never really doubting his father's wisdom. Although he can understand that the physical abuse his friend Liza suffers from her stepfather is wrong, he can't see that his own father's mental and emotional abuse is just as wrong. Cliff, slightly older and more perceptive, is beginning to defy his father.

A thread running throughout the book is Rock's love of history and his positive relationship with the school librarian who encourages his study of the American Revolution. The allusions to the boys being like the American rebels is apparent enough for young readers not used to symbolism to "get it" but not so obvious as to be off-putting to more sophisticated readers.

When Rock doesn't come home for supper one night, his father punishes him by tearing up all his note cards for his paper on the American Revolution. The instances of cruelty continue to add up, slowly, inexorably, until finally Cliff announces they're all going to leave the dad behind and go to Arizona to stay with their mother's sister. Although Rock is not quite ready to buy into this escape plan, Cliff and the mother and younger sister are going even if it means leaving Rock behind. Cliff has deliberately torn off some shingles and while the dad is on the roof fixing them, they plan to escape. In an incredible last scene, Rock is torn between the two sides of his family, between his love for and loyalty to his dad and choosing a new and better life for himself.

"Everyone he'd known had always been right there in reach...It was worse than frightening, the idea of being left behind...Worse than losing his arms or legs. Worse than anything he'd ever known before. He was not a betrayer. He was a patriot, he was a Kindle...Rock had always thought he'd know immediately which side to choose if he were asked to fight. But how could he know where he belonged when the battle lines were being drawn inside his own family?" Here lies the heart of this engaging story and the terrible conflict Rock faces. In the end he chooses to leave, even though that means accepting the truth about his father. It's probably the toughest decision he'll ever make, but he chooses freedom from abuse and a new life for himself.

Griffin does an especially good job on the dialogue and on slowly building the psychological suspense.

TEACHING IDEA

In *Sons of Liberty* Rock longs to be accepted by his father. Two interesting autobiographical pieces on a similar theme are found in *When I Was Your Age: Original Stories About Growing Up* edited by Amy Ehrlich. Each story is written by a well known young adult author. In "The Great Rat Hunt," Lawrence Yep tells of having asthma and how he is unable to impress his father with his athletic ability. In a moving story, the father lets the boy know he accepts him for who he is.

James Howe's "Everything Will Be Okay" is about a sensitive boy whose father and older brothers share a code of toughness that he finds difficult to embrace. An incident when a beloved kitten must be put to death forces him to choose the kind of man he is to become.

Try reading aloud one or both of the stories and discussing how the fathers compare to those in the novels students have read.

• Following in My Own Footsteps

Mary Downing Hahn fans will love *Following in My Own Footsteps,* a novel similar in theme to *Sons of Liberty,* but more accessible to less able middle grade readers. Gordy is a sixth grade bully who puts up a fierce front to the world while inside he is lonely and hurting. His abusive, alcoholic father is in jail and he, his mother, and siblings have moved in with his grandmother. (Those who have read Hahn's World War II novel, *Stepping on the Cracks,* will recognize Gordy and be interested in watching his growth in this later novel.) As Gordy's mother withdraws more and more from the family, Gordy grows close to his grandmother and to William, the boy next door who has polio. With two people who really care about him, the wall Gordy has built up begins to crumble.

Just as life is starting to look a little better, Gordy's father shows up swearing he's reformed and ready to move the entire family to California. Like Rock in *Sons of Liberty,* Gordy must make a difficult choice. He decides to take Grandma's advice to "learn a different way [than his father's] and to follow his own footsteps. Like Rock, he chooses to break out of the pattern of violence he's known all his life. His mother, on the other hand, is ready to give his father yet another chance. In a heart-wrenching scene, she and the younger children take off with never a backward glance at Gordy and his sister June. Gordy realizes he can make a new life with his grandmother and the book ends with these words, " 'Hey, Grandma,' I shouted. 'I'm home.' And do you know what? It was true. I was home. And happy to be there." Although I found the story somewhat oversimplified, I liked Gordy, and the World War II setting added an interesting dimension to the family saga.

• Ironman

Ironman is a powerful novel in which popular author, Chris Crutcher, also takes a close look at father and son relationships. Crutcher's gritty realism and rough language (what he calls teen's "native tongue") is for mature middle grade readers. A therapist in real life, Crutcher deals with tough issues. I heard him speak several years ago at a workshop, and he talked about how he's seen many broken lives. In his writing, as in therapy, he wants to get at the heart of what people's lives are like and help them to find the courage to change.

Like many of the characters in Crutcher's other books, Bo is a super athlete, pushing his body to the limit. "It's a dance...the rhythm of my feet pounding the pavement or the hard snow, the steely repetitions forcing the weights to the beat of Seger or Springsteen, the hum of the tires as I hammer out another mile, the slapping of my hands on the water in perfect drum cadence – it's a dance."

While the athletic dance is an important element of the book, Crutcher is ultimately interested in the emotional dance, of Bo's coming to terms with his abusive father.

Like Rock in *Sons of Liberty,* Bo Brewster's dad is strict and wants Bo to grow up to be a man. His father runs a sporting goods store and one of the worst things he does is sell a super bike to Bo's competitor in the Yukon Jack triathalon. Bo's girlfriend, Shelley, tells him, "You've lost your dad...A real dad would never stack the deck against you...He's no dad. Baby, you've lost him." But Bo and his dad are locked in a power struggle and neither of them seems able to break out of it. Bo is filled with anger and ends up in an anger management workshop at school. He doesn't think he belongs there but finds kindred spirits in the other angry students who have all been hurt in some way by their parents.

Bo's father wants to teach him to be a man, but it is other characters in the book that teach him the true dimensions of a man. Bo is lucky to have two teachers who care, Mr. Serbousek, who is gay, and Mr. Nak, who leads the anger management class and whom Crutcher himself says is one of his favorite characters. Together, the two men model for Bo that a man can be strong and caring at the same time.

Mr. Nak also teaches him where his anger comes from. Near the end, in one of Bo's many letters throughout the book to Larry King, he writes, "It has taken a long time for me to understand Mr. Nak's notion that my anger is cover for my fear, and only when I admit to that fear will I get control of my anger, or in fact have no need for it. I am coming to understand that the fear comes from feeling inadequate when Redmond or my dad pushes me and if I can acknowledge it there's no need to cover it."

We discover that Mr. Nak, through a tragedy in his own life (he killed his children while driving drunk) has had to learn to forgive himself. He passes on the wisdom he's gained the hard way to Bo when he says, "The nature of mercy allows for all things. It excuses nothing, but it allows for all things…Life has every kind of holy man an' devil. If you're ever gonna beat all the anger an' hurt inside you, you're gonna have to learn to offset the awful with the magnificent. But that requires allowin' for both to have their place in the world." At the end of the novel, we feel that Bo has indeed learned a lot about his relationship with his father and, more importantly, so have we. It's not an easy book, but one well worth the effort for mature readers. A group of students who read it and discussed it with me were fascinated by the psychological aspects and went on to read other books by Crutcher.

TEACHING IDEA

The fathers in *Sons of Liberty* and *Ironman* are similar in professing that they want their sons to be "tough." Here's a writing project for pairs of students who have read one of these books. Ask one student to play the part of the father and one to be the son. Have them write a letter to each other in which they express their true feelings toward the other. Encourage them to express their anger, fears, and longings. After receiving and reading the letter they should write a response, attempting to stay in character. It might also be interesting to have them switch places and write from the other's point of view.

• Kinship

My students were making lists of questions they had about their own lives. What kind of job will I have? Who will I marry? When will I die? I saw these questions appear on list after list as I circled the classroom. Then I noticed Tom's paper. "Will I be like my father?" "That's an interesting one," I whispered to him.

"I don't *want* to be like him," he whispered back with great conviction in his voice and expression.

"I understand what you mean," I said, and I moved on, making a mental note to talk to him more about this another time.

In *Kinship,* Trudy Krisher explores this concern that many middle grade students ponder as they consider who they are. Can I untangle myself from my parents' personalities and become my own person? Set in the small community of Kinship, Georgia, in the early 1960s, *Kinship* has a universal appeal and a main character who sparks your interest from the very beginning. Pert Wilson, age 15, lives in Happy Trails Trailer Park, with her mother, Rae Jean, and her older brother, Jimmy, and carries the weight of the world on her shoulders. The family barely scratches out a living. Pert doesn't remember her father who disappeared fifteen years ago, but she longs to see him and get to know him. And then one day he shows up on the doorstep.

At first, Pert is caught up in the thrill of getting to know her daddy. The discerning reader discovers right away that he's a slick talking man, long on charm and short on carry through. But Pert is charmed by his love for adventure and by his disdain for following routines. He sets up a struggle within Pert from the beginning. "…he told me how much he liked how wild I was. 'Clever and wild' was how he put it." Pert begins to notice how different her father and mother are from each other. Rae Jean plays life safe. She doesn't believe in taking risks. She isn't interested in Pert's daddy's offer of a new mobile home in which the entire family can travel the country. Pert is quite sure that her own personality is exactly like her daddy's.

Soon Pert is questioning her family's routines and values. Most of all she is feeling more and more conflict with her mother. When Daddy buys the family a TV, Rae Jean isn't sure she wants to keep it. Pert yells at her mother. "Can't you see that he's just trying to bring some *fun* into your life? …To make you *happy*?"

Rae Jean replies, "People make their own happiness, Pert…It doesn't come out of a TV."

But Pert is in no mood to deal with reason. "The flames was so hot my eyeballs was melting. I was so mad I was blind. Rae Jean was dull as dishwater. She couldn't change. She was stuck."

At the same time that Krisher skillfully reveals Pert's inner life, she also develops another plot line. The residents of the trailer park are being threatened with eviction so the zoning board can turn the area into permanent housing. The residents fight back, and Pert's daddy stays to help. They put metal skirts on their trailers and when that doesn't satisfy the zoning board, they pour concrete around the trailers. They clean up the entire park and even re-name it "Homestead Circle Park: Where the neighbors is just like kin." One of the clever touches Krisher added to this book is the way a resident talks and dispels various types of wisdom for a page or two at the beginning of each chapter. The rest of the time, Pert is the narrator. Each resident is an eccentric character from Sophie Mulch, former school teacher, to Ora and Ida Weevil who run a gambling business out of their trailer and sell spells and potions on the side.

But as Pert's daddy said, she is indeed clever, and her mother has given her a firm set of morals. As she gets to know her daddy better, she begins to realize that he's not quite the knight in shining armor that she had first thought. First, he stands her up for the father-daughter dance. Then she discovers he sold metal skirts to other trailer parks but never delivered them. The shiny, sparkly ring he gave her begins to lose its shine as she discovers what kind of person he really is.

If Pert's daddy is a con man then what kind of person is Pert herself? And what is the difference between *kin* and *family*? These are the questions at the heart of this novel. Pert discovers that she must form her own values. And Krisher makes it very clear that kin are the people you're related to, but family are the people you can trust, the people who will help keep you safe. These are both powerful lessons told in a story vivid with details and feelings and designed to make middle grade readers think about some of life's harder issues.

• The Great Gilly Hopkins
• Out of Nowhere

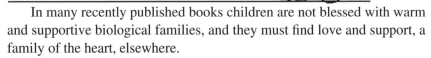

In many recently published books children are not blessed with warm and supportive biological families, and they must find love and support, a family of the heart, elsewhere.

I have long been a fan of Vermont author Katherine Paterson who won the prestigious Hans Christian Anderson Medal in 1988 for the body of her work. Gilly, the main character of *The Great Gilly Hopkins* and one of Paterson's earliest heroines (1978), is also a wounded spirit from the familial battlefield. Her mother, Courtney, abandoned her at three, and Gilly has been a foster child, bumped around from one family to the next ever since. At eleven, with multiple emotional scars, she has constructed a nasty façade to keep people out. She says of herself, "…I am not nice. I am brilliant. I am famous across this entire county. Nobody wants to tangle with the great Galadriel Hopkins. I am too clever and too hard to manage. Gruesome Gilly, they call me…Here I come Maime baby, ready or not."

But Maime Trotter, Gilly's new foster mom, is ready for anyone, her huge love ready to enfold Gilly as it already has William Ernest, her other foster child. William Ernest, too, is ready to love and accept Gilly. Mr. Randolph, a frail Black man who lives next door and eats at Maime's, completes the cast of characters.

When Gilly's attempt to run away from Maime's fails, she writes to her mother and paints a bleak picture of her life. But even as she waits desperately for a letter from Courtney, her own feelings begin to change. She feels a kinship with Mr. Randolph as she reads poetry to him. She teaches W.E. how to defend himself and the two grow closer. When everyone else comes down with a bad case of the flu, Gilly nurses them back to health. She has, despite herself, become a part of this "family."

But Paterson is too realistic to end the story here with a happily-ever-after finish. As a result of Gilly's letter to her mother, she is shipped off to live with Nonnie, her grandmother. When her mother shows up for Christmas, Gilly loses the last of her illusions about the beautiful and perfect mother she'd created in her mind. "She hadn't come because she wanted to. She'd come because Nonnie had paid her to. And she wasn't going to stay. And she wasn't going to take Gilly back with her. 'I will always love you.' It was a lie. Gilly had thrown away her whole life for a stinking lie." This is not an easy truth for someone of any age to accept and Gilly's first instinct is to run back to Maime.

But Maime confirms what Gilly has just figured out. "…all that stuff about happy endings is lies…Life ain't supposed to be nothing, 'cept maybe tough." Maime says you can't expect good things all the time. No one owes you a good life. "Nothing to make you happy like doing good on a tough job…" And Gilly's tough job is to stay with her grandmother. "Your grandma is home," says Maime. Gilly has gained the strength to accept these words of wisdom from Maime. She is no longer the obnoxious self-absorbed brat she was when the story opened. She can accept Maime's words of wisdom and get on with her life.

Kirsten, a sixth grader who really enjoyed this book found it sad "because Gilly had to go to all kinds of foster homes, and her real mom never wanted her. This book was sad, but it had a good ending." Paterson's ending is satisfying because its message is so strong and clear. We are each responsible for our own happiness. Despite the mistakes of our biological parents we all have a choice of starting anew and creating our own life.

Harley, the main character in Ouida Sebestyen's *Out of Nowhere,* also needs to start over and make a new life for himself. His mother takes off with her latest boyfriend and leaves 13-year-old Harley in the middle of the Arizona desert. "Could this really happen?" I asked a group of my students who had read the book. "These things happen in today's world. You'd be surprised!" one boy said. The others nodded.

Harley meets up with 69-year-old May, whose husband has left her after 40 years of marriage, and together they set off to her childhood home where she hopes to start a new life. There they meet Bill, a relentless collector who has been renting May's house and refuses to move out, and Singer, a young woman who moves around helping out those in need. Added to this collection of eccentrics is Ish, a pit bull who has been dumped in the middle of the desert by his owners and whom Harley has adopted.

Together this mismatched team begins cleaning and painting May's house. Harley does not know much about love or being part of a family, and each of the characters try to teach him to work cooperatively, to be responsible for Ish, and to let go of the hurt caused by his mother's neglect. May, too, is deeply wounded, and both she and Harley slowly begin to heal and trust each other. They agree to start "practice feeling loved," and although Singer leaves at the end, Bill, May, Harley, and their assorted animals are going to try being a family.

Sebestyen has created a memorable cast of characters and just the right mix of emotion and action. "But can you relate to a book where the situation is so different from your own family?" I asked my students, most of whom come from a middle-class family with a mother, father, and one or two siblings. "I think you can relate to the feelings," said Anna thoughtfully. "Plus, in real life, you never know what other families are like. You only know your own family, so it's really interesting to see how other families get along." An eighth grader wrote about one reason why she liked the book:

"When the people in the book reacted to things, I could somehow relate to that situation. When Harley stormed off and wouldn't get into the car I could relate to his feelings because sometimes when I get really mad at my parents, I storm off and feel just like how the author describes Harley feeling."

Whether it is a biological family or a family whose members have found each other and chosen to be together, a healthy family is built on a foundation of trust and acceptance. None of the members are perfect. They make mistakes. They feel regret. But if they can love and forgive and go on, then the family will thrive.

TEACHING IDEA

Many of the books in this chapter would make interesting selections for a Parents and Students Read Together evening. (See Appendix A for tips on organizing such an evening.) The complex relationships between parents and children that are a central theme in these novels should lead to interesting dialogue.

If I were to select a few novels to offer for such an evening that would likely lead to spirited discussion, I'd choose *Tangerine, Sons of Liberty* (for easier reading), *Ironman,* and *One Bird* (for more challenging reading).

In each of the books in this chapter, young adolescents come to see their parents as individuals, to forgive them for their mistakes, and, finally, to fly from the nest and build lives of their own. They are among the most believable and likable characters you will meet in young adult literature. In these books, there is no oversimplification. There is no hiding the pain of adolescence. But woven into the fabric of each novel is a sense of the strength and support a loving family, whether biological or of the heart, provides as a child moves toward independence.

Those who read are some of the luckiest people in the world since they can travel all over the earth and stay put at the same time. — Emily Smith, Grade 6

Chapter 3: When Danger Threatens
— *Novels about survival* —

D anger threatens. Security is shaken. Life hangs in the balance. The temptation is strong to give up, give in, retreat, or hide. Somewhere in the thick of the suspense, the characters reach deep down inside and find qualities they did not know existed. They had never needed them before, but they are there, and as they use them, their confidence grows. They learn they can trust their judgment, their skills, their courage. This is a strength they can count on for life.

These are the elements of most survival stories. Think of the monumentally popular *Hatchet* by Gary Paulsen. It is the one my students thought of first when I asked what survival books they had read. This was closely followed by *Island of the Blue Dolphins* by Scott O'Dell, *Julie of the Wolves* by Jean St. George, and *The Iceberg Hermit* by Arthur Roth.

In each of these books, which are classic wilderness survival tales, the main character is alone in the wilderness struggling to reach safety. The settings vary, from deep woods, to deserted islands, to the frigid Arctic; but in each case there are no adults who know what to do. There is only a young, untried person pitted against elements and obstacles that seem insurmountable.

There are hundreds of books that could be classified as survival stories. Although the settings and the situations vary, the basics of danger and finding the strength to overcome it are present in each. Let's look at some of the best in this broad genre.

- **The River**
- **Brian's Winter**
- **Brian's Return**

Gary Paulsen's three sequels to *Hatchet* are all good reads. In *The River,* which is my least favorite of the three, Brian returns to the wilderness on a canoe trip with a psychiatrist who wants to study the psychological effects of extreme survival conditions. I have so much trouble believing that

Brian's parents would ever agree to this that it nearly ruined the book for me. Students have enjoyed it, but most feel it's not as good as *Hatchet.*

In *Brian's Winter,* which Paulsen refers to as an "alternate sequel," he imagines what would have happened if Brian had not been rescued and had been forced to face a winter alone in the North woods. In his typical fashion, Paulsen keeps the action moving as Brian faces one difficult test after another. Cormick, a sixth grade boy, found it "an all around good book." He was interested in the psychological difficulties of surviving alone. "I think Brian is on the verge of going crazy. Picture it, being without anyone to talk to, alone in the wilderness. Actually, I was surprised that he didn't totally lose his mind."

The final story about Brian, *Brian's Return,* is a different sort of book from the other three. Brian has returned to civilization and is having trouble adjusting to ordinary life. Although he tries hard to be normal, the activities and conversations of his friends hold no interest for him, and the noise of modern life is a constant irritant. He feels empty and longs for the solitude and beauty, the realness of the wilderness. In the second half of the book, Brian returns to the North woods to take a long canoe trip by himself. In this book Paulsen is far less interested in building a suspenseful plot. He writes long passages describing the beauty of the wilderness – sunsets and starlit nights, loons calling, and mice making homes under the snow. In great detail he describes the equipment Brian takes with him. Although there are some suspenseful scenes, encounters with a deer, a bear, and a storm, Paulsen seems interested in Brian's emotional and spiritual survival rather than the edge of death experiences he describes in his other books. Brian is trying to figure out what to do with his life. Where does he belong? He reads Shakespeare aloud by the edge of a lake. He meets an old woodsman named Billy and "...it hit him that when he'd met Billy he was meeting himself years from now, an old man who looked carved in wood moving through and with the forest, being of and with the woods, and he decided that it wouldn't be so bad a thing to be." Students who are ardent Paulsen fans enjoyed this book and bemoaned the fact that Paulsen says it's the last book he'll write about Brian.

• GUTS

However, Paulsen has written a non-fiction book that students who loved the *Brian* series or who are interested in wilderness survival will find fascinating. *GUTS* contains "the true stories behind *Hatchet* and the *Brian* books." Paulsen explains that because he wanted everything that happened to Brian to be based on reality, he decided to write only about experiences he had actually had himself.

He tells about surviving a moose that was stomping on him and how badly he wanted to kill that moose. He tells about his experiences with mosquitoes and convinced me that I never want to hike in a northern area with vicious mosquitoes. Even as he spins fascinating true tales of danger in the wilderness, he explains the importance of knowledge as a survival tool. "The solution to facing all these dangers, a solution that came very rapidly to me and to Brian, is knowledge. It can come from anywhere; from reading, from listening to people, or from personal experience. However it comes, the knowledge must be there."

He talks about different methods of wilderness cooking and how when you're starving, you'll eat anything from fish eyeballs to grub worms wrapped in dandelion greens. One of the longest chapters in the book is called, "Killing to Live: Hunting and Fishing with Primitive Weapons." Paulsen relates his experiences growing up, how he made his own bow and arrows, and how he spent two days dragging a buck that weighed twice as much as he did, out of a swamp and six miles home.

What is especially interesting about *GUTS* is that not only are the stories true but he explains how he used his own experiences to create a much loved novel. But perhaps what I like best about the book is how it illustrates one of the truths that is woven into the *Brian* books. "To learn, to be willing to learn how a thing works, to understand an animal in nature, or how to write a book or run a dog team, or sail a boat, to always keep learning is truly wonderful."

TEACHING IDEA

For students who are trying to write fiction it is important for them to see that they can use their own experiences as part of a fictional tale. An excellent way to illustrate this to middle grade writers is to read aloud the beginning of *Hatchet* where the plane crashes. Then read aloud the first chapter of *GUTS*, "Heart Attacks, Plane Crashes, and Flying." Although Paulsen never actually crashed in a plane, he tells numerous stories and explains how he pieced together these experiences to write with authority about Brian's plane crash.

• Dogsong

Gary Paulsen has written another survival novel that, in many ways, is as good as his series about Brian. *Dogsong* is the story of Russel Suskitt, a 14-year-old Eskimo who leaves behind the modern ways of his village and journeys into the Arctic on a quest for his true self. Like the characters in most of the books I've described so far, the young person undertakes a journey, is tested, comes close to failure, perseveres, and discovers in the end the strength and courage that lie within.

Russel feels uncomfortable with the modern ways his village has adopted, especially the widespread use of snowmobiles. He realizes it is really himself he's unhappy with, and in his search for answers, he goes to Oogruk, a wise elder. Oogruk inspires him to find his own song, to become his song, to return to the right ways of living. He teaches him much of what he knows, and Russel learns to drive Oogruk's team of dogs. Paulsen does a masterful job describing the dogs and the art of dogsledding in language that is close to poetry. "The feeling, he thought, the feeling is that the sled is alive; that I am alive and the sled is alive and the snow is alive and the ice is alive and we are all part of the same life."

In one of the many exciting scenes in this book, Russel and the dogs are out on the ice during a storm. They survive the storm only to head off in the wrong direction because the huge plate of ice they were on had rotated during the storm. He figures out the problem and heads toward home only to come up against a strip of open water too wide to see across." This is typical Paulsen – one crisis after another to keep the reader flipping those pages!

Oogruk, knowing that his time to die has come, has Russel take him out on the ice and leave him by the edge of the sea. He tells Russel to "...head north and take meat and see the country. When you do that you will become a man. Run as long as you can. That's what used to be.... Run with the dogs and become what the dogs will help you become." And so Russel sets forth on his journey.

Part II is titled "The Dreamrun," and for several chapters Paulsen alternates between the run Russel is making across the land to the north and the dream he has of a man who is himself in a former, prehistoric life. "The dream had folded into his life and his life had folded back into the dream so many times that it was not possible for him to find which was real and which was dream."

He finds a half frozen young woman who is pregnant, and he takes her along on his journey. Paulsen seems to be saying that part of becoming a man is learning compassion, how to reach out to others. They run out of food, there are no animals or tracks for many days, and they come close to death. Finally, Russel kills a great polar bear in a climactic scene that seems his final test of manhood.

In Part III we read his song, Dogsong, which ends with these words:

Come, see my dogs.
> Out before me they go.
> Out before me they curve
> in the long line out
> before me
> they go, I go, we go. They are me.

Over the years, many of my students have read and enjoyed this book. They've been intrigued by an ancient way of life so different from their own and moved by Russel's courage and strength as he becomes a man. Some have even decided to write their own song!

• The Cay
• Far North

The Cay by Theodore Taylor is another classic survival tale. I've used it successfully several times as a book for parents and students to read together and discuss. The book is set in the Caribbean during World War II. When the boat Phillip and his mother are traveling on is torpedoed by the Germans, Phillip finds himself on a raft with Timothy, an old West Indian man. He's grown up believing that Black people are inferior and his prejudice is very apparent. To make things worse, a blow to the head leaves Phillip blind and dependent on Timothy. They land on a small cay and Timothy teaches Phillip about building a shelter and finding food. He refuses to let Phillip sink into self pity and forces him to become more self-reliant despite his blindness.

Timothy is worried that they might never be rescued. He's old and fears he may die soon and so he works harder to prepare Phillip to be completely self-reliant. Phillip and Timothy's relationship gradually changes and Phillip grows to love and respect Timothy.

They survive a terrible hurricane together. Shortly after the hurricane Timothy dies and Phillip is left alone. If this had happened earlier in the story, I doubt that Phillip would have had the skills or courage to live alone, but Timothy has taught him well. When he is finally rescued at the end of the book, he has the confidence that comes from being tested and passing the test.

This is not a difficult book although some readers may have a little trouble adjusting to Timothy's dialect. The message is straightforward and easy for younger middle school readers to figure out.

TEACHING IDEA

An interesting way to help students find the theme of the book is to have them pretend that at the end of the book the main character makes a poster to hang over his or her bed. The poster should contain a message that sums up what the character has learned from the survival adventure. Students could actually create such a poster as an advertisement for their book illustrating it with the setting or an important scene as well as the message. If your students are all reading different survival stories, decorating the room with these posters is a good way to share books and give students ideas for other books they might enjoy.

For many years, I've thought of *Hatchet* as the definitive outdoor survival story. But recently, I decided that *Far North* by Will Hobbs gives *Hatchet* a run for its money. It is one of the best outdoor adventures I've read. Perhaps reading it as the snow blew against my window during the middle of a Vermont winter storm helped to set the mood. But I think Hobbs sets the mood quite well without any assistance from the Vermont weather.

Gabe, a 15-year-old from Texas, is going to school in the Northwest Territories because his father is working there on diamond exploration, and Raymond, his roommate who is from a remote Dene village, are stranded in the wilderness with a Dene elder, Johnny Raven. It's December on the Nahanni river, a sub-Arctic world of ice, snow, temperatures that fall below negative 60 degrees, and the animals that inhabit this beautiful but dangerous land.

They learn about survival from Johnny Raven, but when he suddenly dies, they must put all he has taught them into practice. As the narrator, Gabe reveals his feelings without overdoing it. "I was shivering, more from fear, I think, than from the cold...try to be brave, I told myself. This is when it really counts. I could hear my mother telling me how strong I was, how tough. She always said that. I didn't feel strong at all. I felt more like crying."

When the boys kill a moose, they decide that Gabe will pull part of the moose back to the cabin, several days journey, while Raymond stays with the rest. It's a very difficult trip for Gabe. The temperature falls below minus 60 degrees. At one point he walks into some slush and almost freezes his feet and hands. He knows that if he's unable to move his hands, he'll be unable to light a fire, and then he'll freeze to death. Only through quick thinking and action is he able to save himself.

Hobbs describes the beauty of the North well. "In the afternoon twilight the cold deepened. The trees were freezing and splitting, and the streambeds made an eerie drumming **spaaaaaang** that resounded away under the ice…when the twilight was gone I kept pulling by the surreal blazing-cold white light of the full moon, in and out of the long timber shadows. Far off, two owls were talking across the frozen stillness."

Gabe and Raymond finally get the meat back to the cabin only to encounter a "winter bear," a grizzly that didn't put on enough fat to hibernate. They narrowly escape getting killed by the grizzly, but are unable to save most of their moose meat. With only a small supply of meat left, they decide to try to hike down the frozen Nahanni River. Raymond is, by now, unable to walk, and he tries to persuade Gabe to go without him. Gabe refuses in a moving tribute to their friendship. "I won't even think about it…You're the best friend I'm ever going to have. I've just been hearing about what your mother said how life is the greatest gift. She's right. That's why we've been trying so hard to stay alive. But friendship, that's as close to the top of the list as you can get."

And so they set off together, "going for broke," as Gabe says. They make it over an ice bridge, another danger that could kill them in an instant if it cracked and broke. When the two friends pull into Raymond's village, there were tears in my eyes. I was so happy they'd made it. The book doesn't end here but rather at a potlatch, a ceremony to celebrate Johnny Raven's life. Raymond reads the letter Johnny left with them and ends with the words, "…take care of the land, take care of yourself, take care of each other." This is clearly Hobbs' message to his readers.

Before recommending this book to your students you should be aware that there are two deaths. One is Johnny Raven's. He dies of an apparent heart attack, and the boys find him lying in the snow. He's an old man and he's been sick before this, so his death, while sad, is not unexpected. The second is that of the young pilot who flies them into the wilderness. He is swept over Virginia Falls to his death in a frightening scene early in the adventure.

What I liked so much about this book is that it is not just adventure built around one dangerous situation after another although there certainly is enough suspense for most young readers. There's also the rich friendship between the two boys as well as their relationship with Johnny Raven before he dies. There's the way they have to think clearly and how one mistake, one wrong decision can easily end their lives. They must use all the reasoning skills they possess. And even then, good or bad luck can determine their fate. Hobbs has also written other survival stories that your students might enjoy such as *Downriver,* its sequel *River Thunder,* and *The Maze.*

• Between a Rock and a Hard Place

Between a Rock and a Hard Place is a riveting survival story by Alden R. Carter.

Take one slightly overweight teenager with zero self-confidence. Add another with diabetes, not much more confidence than the first, and no experience in the outdoors. Then put these two cousins in the wilderness of northern Minnesota on a camping and canoeing trip that has been a tradition in their family for two generations. What you get is a very interesting story.

A reader needs some patience before he gets to the riveting part. The first 100 pages unwind slowly as Mark and Randy set off reluctantly into the wilderness. They aren't crazy about this "coming-of-age-experience" their parents have pressured them into, and they aren't too fond of each other. During the long days of canoeing, there's not much to do besides talk. While much of their conversation is irritatingly self-pitying, they gradually start to open up to each other about things that are important in their lives. Mark shares his feelings about being a huge disappointment to his family, of never measuring up to his older brother, Bob. "Just imagine trying to follow someone like Bob through school. Every teacher who ever had him expects me to be just like him: brain, jock, president of this, captain of that. But I get them over that quick. I'm not my big brother, and I don't want to be." Rather than compete, Mark has given up his love of art, given up trying in school; he's settled into being a failure.

Randy talks about having to convince his parents that diabetes doesn't mean he can't be independent and lead a full life. He tells Mark that his parents are on the verge of divorce and only waiting to see if he can do well on this trip. "This is the big test. If I do okay, they can say: 'Okay, the

wimp's old enough to make it on his own. So pass the divorce papers...'
When I finally prove I'm no wimp, that's when they split up."

The silence and beauty of the lake and forest start to work their magic, and the boys gain confidence as the days slide by. Just when I had begun to wonder if this was really a survival story, things started to go wrong. The pace accelerates, and the second half of the book is a real page-turner. First, a bear gets most of their food, and the instrument that Randy uses to measure his blood sugar level doesn't seem to be working properly. Still, they figure they can make the food they have last for the two day trip back to the lodge where their fathers are waiting for them.

Then the canoe drifts away, and Mark makes a heroic swim to rescue it. No sooner have they continued on their journey than they make a bad decision. Hoping to save time, they choose to shoot a series of rapids rather than do the portages. They go through the first two fairly easy rapids fine, but when they come to Class II rapids, they wreck the canoe and lose most of their gear, including Randy's insulin. As they attempt to walk back to the lodge, Randy gets weaker and weaker. When he falls into a diabetic coma, Mark struggles on alone hoping to get help in time. His bad luck is almost not believable, but by now you care so much about his making it that you hardly notice. He runs into an impenetrable swamp and has to retrace his steps. He swims a channel and loses his boots. He breaks his collar bone when he's washed over a waterfall, and still he keeps going. When he finally stumbles into the lodge, you'll either be cheering with joy or crying with relief, or maybe both. It all ends happily with Mark a hero, his life turned around, and Randy planning their trip for next summer. But on the way to this satisfying ending there's plenty of time for the reader to wonder if he'd have had the courage that Mark did to keep going in the face of seemingly insurmountable obstacles.

• Frozen Stiff

Frozen Stiff by Sherry Shahan is a straightforward survival story that will appeal to younger middle school readers. Too many survival stories feature boys as the main character, and I like the fact that a young girl plays that role in this book. Cody and her cousin Derek set off on a two night camping and kayaking trip into the Alaskan wilderness while their mothers are away. Two nights of freedom paddling down the steep-sided fjord sounds like a great adventure to the two cousins. Just how big a risk are they taking? Although Cody has had experience kayaking she knew that no trips were scheduled this late in the summer. Students should have a lively debate about the wisdom of the initial decision. Is it a risk they would take?

At first, the challenges are manageable. Strenuous paddling in places, the difficulty of finding a campsite, and even an encounter with a black bear keep the plot moving steadily forward. But suddenly during their first night of camping, the water in Russell Fjord begins to rise, and Cody's kayak and life vest are swept away. Hubbard Glacier has surged and its advance cuts off the mouth of the fjord. Not only have they lost Cody's kayak. The water purifier, sunscreen, insect repellent, and most of the food are also gone.

Things get even worse the next day when Cody, without her sunglasses, is temporarily blinded. For two days Derek takes care of her as she floats in and out of consciousness.

One of the things I especially like about Shahan's writing is that she keeps the action moving at a rapid pace. For students who are not crazy about reading, this is a good book to catch their interest! There's also an interesting subplot about Cody's parents' divorce and her anger and hurt that her father left and remarried.

Just as one problem is solved, another appears. Cody regains her sight and is hopeful that a rescue party is on its way. That hope disappears when she learns that Derek tore up the note she left for her mother. He'd been afraid someone would find it before they left and ruin their adventure.

Then Derek disappears, and Cody believes that he has been kidnapped by a poacher. She follows their tracks through the wilderness only to discover that the poacher is not a poacher and that Derek has gone with the man and his wife voluntarily. At first she is wary and unwilling to trust these people, but gradually, as she hears their story and realizes they've saved both hers and Derek's life, she's won over.

The theme is in plain sight for younger readers to grasp easily. As Cody and Derek leave the camp of their rescuers and head for the glacier where there will be people to take them home, Derek thanks Cody for bringing him on the kayaking trip.

"We came through for each other," she said, remembering her snow blindness. "When it counted most."

"Nothing will ever be the same, said Derek…"Everything is different."

Cody knew what he meant. They were different because of all they'd been through. "Do you know what the outfitters call an adventure?"

"What?"

"An experience outside your comfort zone," she said.

Derek smiled. "We had an adventure, Cody."

They have faced danger and found the courage and strength within themselves to survive. The reader who went along for the ride cannot help but wonder if he or she would have discovered the same toughness within.

• The Sacrifice

The Sacrifice by Diane Matcheck is another excellent novel with a feminine heroine. It is the coming-of-age saga of a 15-year-old Apsaalooka Indian girl in mid-18th century America. She finds herself lost and on her own in the vast wilderness that today is Montana. She has been shunned all her life by her own people and burdened by guilt that she had caused her brother's death. When her father dies she sets off to prove herself to her people but ends up lost instead. Each chapter brings new dangers. In a very graphic scene she fights a grizzly bear for her life and survives. This heroic act gives her new confidence in herself. "All doubt had fled…she was the Great One, the one who would number among the greatest Apsaalooka ever to live. Who could doubt it, after she had killed a grizzly bear! Alone, half-starved, half-crippled, with nothing but a knife she had killed it. No, she was not Weak-one-who-does-not-last. She could do anything now…. Her wounds from this ordeal would fade away. But her pride would live forever." Passing this test gives her confidence, but it does not erase the years of being an outcast or the bitterness this caused. It takes the friendship and acceptance of a Pawnee boy to do that.

Shortly after she kills the bear, she is captured by Pawnees and taken a long distance to their homeland. Little does she know that she is to be the sacrifice in an ancient ceremony to satisfy the Morning Star. A young boy is put in charge of her and must prevent her from escaping. Gradually, they become friends, then the friendship deepens to love. The boy, Wolfstar, teaches her to laugh, and sing, and enjoy life. She feels safe in the warmth of his friendship. Soon she learns about the sacrifice and realizes the boy she loves is going to allow her to be killed.

An interesting note from the author at the end of the book explains that the Morning Star sacrifice had been part of the Pawnee ritual for many, many years and only ended in 1817, when the son of a Pawnee chief rescued a girl from the altar as she was about to be killed.

As in the historical event, Wolfstar rescues her at the last minute, and they escape together. But in yet another twist of the plot, his father kills him for helping her. The girl is grief-stricken and considers ending her own life. But she realizes that Wolfstar had died to save her and that she must make something of her life. "She did not know how she would do it, but this new sense of purpose filled her as nothing had ever filled her before.... As she turned away she felt light. Full of light. There was a fire in her...a steady, rare, red-gold flame. And suddenly she knew her name. Somewhat lightened of her burdens, Grizzlyfire descended the great bluff, mounted her horse, and turned toward home." She travels on alone back to her own people to try to make a new life.

This book, especially in the beginning, has all the suspense of *Hatchet*. The girl is an interesting character and although she is not always likeable, the reader comes to understand her, and I found myself rooting for her survival. When she discovers she is to be the sacrifice, it's quite shocking. It's even more shocking when Wolfstar dies. This is not a happy-ever-after story even though it has a positive and hopeful ending. It is not a book for younger middle school readers. The scene where she kills the grizzly is quite graphic, and the idea of human sacrifice may be too shocking to less mature readers. Matcheck's description is excellent and evokes another time period very well.

• The Place of Lions

In *The Place of Lions*, Eric Campbell writes not only a fast-paced survival story but one that describes the beauty of Africa as well. Chris and his father are in a small plane on the way to their new home in Tanzania when the plane crashes in the middle of the Serengetti. The pilot is badly injured, and Chris's father's leg is broken. As Chris recovers from the shock of the crash, he realizes he is the only one able to go for help. He finds himself "in a world where life was stripped down the elemental necessities of all men in all times: food, water, shelter."

As Chris leaves on his dangerous search for help, an old lion who is nearing death and returning to the place of his youth follows him. When Chris encounters a band of ruthless poachers, the old lion intercedes and rescues him. Campbell describes an almost spiritual connection between the lion and the boy. When the lion seems too weak to make it to his final destination, Chris encourages him. "They rose together up the side of the hill, the boy first, the great, slow figure, like a huge, faithful, golden dog, a few feet behind. Two spirits caught and held. Bound in a magic, brief but eternal."

Although Campbell's writing may contain a bit too much description for some middle grade readers, he does a good job of bringing to life a continent that until recently was rarely described in young adult literature. He describes the "vast, heart-stopping emptiness…the great lonelinesses and silences of Africa…" Brenna, a sixth grader liked how Campbell described Chris. "I thought the author gave Chris a lot of courage. When Chris went looking for help, nobody really helped him to survive. He was self-confident and believed that he could make it."

The book includes an interesting subplot about Mike, a tourist guide, Bennie, the Masai who works for him, and an American tourist who stumble onto a grisly scene of poachers chopping off an elephant's tusks. The story alternates between Chris's adventure and the men's pursuit of the poachers. Campbell makes his opinion of the poachers very clear when he describes Mike's "…disgust, his blind anger and hatred of the senseless, mindless slaughter..." This is a book not only about the survival of a young white boy but also about the survival of Africa's wild animals.

The book ends with Bennie explaining that the story of Chris and the lion has become a legend among the Masai. "They know why the *simba* came with you," says Bennie. "…the lion looked at you and saw a heart as brave as his own." Many of my students have enjoyed reading about this brave-hearted boy and imagining themselves in his situation.

TEACHING IDEA

Before reading a survival novel, ask students to imagine that they are going to take a three-month hike in the wilderness. If they could choose only one companion, what qualities would this person have? Some qualities they might want to consider are personality, sex, age, health, intellectual ability, physical strength, attitude, profession, experience. Then ask them to rank order the qualities. This should lead to an interesting discussion as students debate which qualities seem most important to them. After students have read a survival novel, have them return to their list and see if they still feel the same. Those who have read a novel with two characters can discuss which qualities each character most valued in the other.

• Stones in Water

There are many novels about survival during war. One of my favorites is Donna Jo Napoli's *Stones in Water.* Young Roberto faces both the inhumanity of soldiers during war and a bitterly cold Russian winter in his battle to survive. During World War II, boys in Italy, Hungary, Romania, and other Axis nations were taken by the Nazis to work for the war effort. Napoli wrote this novel to bring this little known piece of history to life. She does an admirable job in this fast-paced story.

Roberto has grown up in Venice. The war has not affected him very much until one afternoon he and his older brother and two friends, one of whom is Jewish, go to the theatre. His innocent world is shattered when during the movie, Nazi soldiers march into the theatre and take all the boys away. They are trucked to work camps in German territory to build airstrips and do other back-breaking work. Hunger, cold, and hard labor are their constant companions. Roberto and his friend Samuele manage to stay together and hide the secret that Samuele is Jewish. Napoli has written far more than a survival story. This is a touching story of Roberto and Samuele's friendship and how they manage to keep each other alive.

Napoli has created a realistic picture of the inhumanity people are capable of. There are scenes that contain acts of vicious violence such as when a Nazi soldier shoots a boy in the head. There is unrelenting hardship and situations that nearly result in death. There are bleak scenes of villages where all the people have been shot. Because of this, I would not recommend this book to younger middle school readers, and I would warn older students that it contains some images of violence.

As Samuele lays dying, he makes Roberto promise to fight to stay alive. "You have to fight. I don't mean with your fists. I mean inside. Don't ever let them win over the inside of you." After Samuele dies, Roberto escapes from the work camp which is somewhere in the Ukraine and heads south. The second half of the book is about Roberto's journey toward home. For some of the time he's alone with no food and only a blanket for warmth against the brutal cold of winter. "Night came. There were no trees to burrow under or climb up into. The moon was bright on the snow, so bright Roberto could still follow the soldiers' trail. He kept walking. Whether sleeping or moving, he was a target for whatever might be on the prowl – animal or human. Soldiers."

In a small village where the people have been killed by soldiers, he finds a lone survivor, a young boy, and they travel together for awhile. This relieves Roberto's acute loneliness even though he can't communicate with the boy. When Roberto is taken prisoner the boy helps him escape. Then Roberto is on his own, on the run again.

Eventually, he meets up with an Italian army deserter and together they continue toward Italy where they plan to join the *partigiana,* the Italian resistance. Both have had enough of war and are ready to work for peace. There are many excellent books about WWII, and this is among the best I've read. A group of students who read it during our study of World War II also loved it, and for weeks after the group concluded, I overheard them recommending it to their friends.

> **TEACHING IDEA**
> Ask students to make a list of the problems the character in their survival book had to solve. Encourage them to include mental and emotional problems as well as physical ones. Then check which ones were life or death problems, ones the character would have died for if he hadn't solved them. Have students discuss which problems seemed most challenging to the character. Then have them discuss or write about the ones that would have been hardest for them.

• The Girl Who Owned a City

Not all survival, of course, takes place in the wilderness. In *The Girl Who Owned a City* O.T. Nelson writes a futuristic tale in which everyone over the age of 12 has been killed by a virus. One of my students who reads with great reluctance loved this book and thought that "One of the best things the author did, was make a really unrealistic topic realistic, and it doesn't seem like that's an easy thing to do."

The story begins in a neighborhood where small families of children are struggling to survive. Finding food is their major problem. Lisa, the heroine, uses her intelligence to survive. "The same mind that used to get "A's" in math and English was now struggling to pass a frightening course in survival."

There are many memorable scenes in this book. Lisa bravely drives her father's car to an outlying farm to find food. She makes many return trips at night in complete darkness. She teaches other children to drive, and one night she and her friend Craig have a race at sixty miles an hour down a straight stretch of road. What young adolescent wouldn't love to have the keys to the family car and be able to drive whenever he wanted?

In another scene, Lisa discovers a huge warehouse full of supplies. Then she trades her food with the other children in the neighborhood in return for their forming a militia to defend their homes from gangs bent on looting their supplies. Soon she's organized the entire neighborhood. There are many interesting details of trapdoors in the roofs, booby traps, and trumpet and drum signals if enemies approach.

Lisa is a character who thinks big. She dreams of getting the world working again. When her friend Craig shares his dream of farming, she wonders, "Would they have to live like the people in olden times, spending long days in the fields? Or even worse, would they have to live like those children in really poor places, begging, stealing, and having no time for play? Would they grow old and tired while the jets on the runway rusted and died forever?" She is confident that they can make things work again.

Life seems good until the Chidester gang sneaks in one night and burns down Lisa's home. Lisa's confidence in her own ideas and abilities is momentarily shaken. But she quickly recovers and comes up with a new idea. The children take over a huge, fortress-like school on a hill high above the town. Soon hundreds of other children join them. Once again, Lisa feels invincible. But one stupid mistake is all it takes, and she finds herself wounded by the Chidester gang and left for dead. Again, she bounces back from defeat, learns from her mistakes, and is once again in charge of her city.

It's a simple tale but one that has enormous appeal to middle grade readers. Some of my most reluctant readers have loved this book! The idea of children running their own lives is one that young adolescents never fail to find appealing. I find Nelson's story far too laden with didactic messages about building character through working hard and earning your own way through life's difficulties. Don't get me wrong. I think this is an important message for middle grade students, but I find Nelson's repetitious treatment of it annoying. Apparently, my students had no problem with this, proving once again that kids have their own opinions about books, and they often don't match those of adults. "I want another one just like this," said one girl who, only a few weeks earlier, had told me she hated to read.

• River Rats

River Rats by Caroline Stevermer is another good futuristic novel. The story is set in a post-apocalyptic world after a 21st century disaster has ravaged civilization. "The Flash" followed by riots and disease, has left the survivors in small groups eking out a living the best they can. Tom Cat and his five friends survive on the ***River Rat***, an old paddle wheel steamboat they "liberated." Together they travel up and down the Mississippi River delivering mail and making music for the people at the small towns along the way in exchange for food.

The action moves swiftly throughout the book from the first chapter where the Rats rescue an old man who's being pursued by a gang of tough looking thugs. The old man, King, brings them trouble as the thugs, known as the Lesters, continue their hunt for him. They believe he knows where a supply of guns from the old days is stored, and they're determined to get the guns. At last, they board the steamboat and take over, threatening to kill the kids one by one unless King takes them to the guns. Leaving one Rat behind as a hostage, King, the rest of the kids, and one Lester set off to find the guns and bring them back. They have just seven days to accomplish their mission.

In a smooth plot twist, Stevermer reveals that King is really The Pharaoh, a very famous rock musician just before The Flash. The guns and other supplies are stored in a special tomb that the Pharaoh used his royalties to build. The trip to the tomb is fraught with danger from the pestilence that kills the Lester to the Wild Boys who roam the ruined city they must past through and who capture them. The description of the ruined city and the scenes with the Wild Boys who live in a parking garage with one old Mercedes is one of the best parts of the book. The Wild Boys want Tom Cat to join their gang, and it makes an interesting small group discussion to see what decision students would make if faced with a similar dilemma.

King and the River Rats manage to escape from the Wild Boys and find the tomb only to discover that like the Pharaoh's tombs of ancient times, it has already been looted, and the guns are gone. Now they must figure out a way to convince the Lesters to give them back the ***River Rat*** even though they have no guns to give in return.

The pace is fast, and the problems the Rats face change to keep the book interesting. Students will enjoy it and probably won't care that there is very little character development. Each of the five main characters are distinctive personalities but we never really get to know them beyond their tough exterior image. You might consider having some students compare the character development in *River Rats* with that in *Tomorrow When the War Began*. The contrast is quite striking and could lead to a good analytical discussion. Does it matter that there isn't much character development? Is the fact that the book has a fast moving and exciting plot enough, or could *River Rats* have been a better novel with character development?

Regardless of the outcome of the discussion, it's a good book to recommend to students and Stevermer describes both the post-apocalyptic world and the camaraderie of life on the river equally well. As Tom Cat says, "Living on a paddle wheel steamboat is like living in a house that moves, yet it sometimes seems to be the one thing in the world that holds still. You feel the deck alive beneath you while the river unwinds all around you. It's life. That's what: the only life for me."

TEACHING IDEA

For a source of short stories to read aloud or use for whole class discussion and analysis, try *Read for Your Life: Tales of Survival,* a collection compiled by the editors of *Read Magazine.* There are many excellent stories, some by well-known authors such as Gary Paulsen and Jack London. The collection is designed for reluctant readers with stories that are particularly suspenseful. The stories are organized into three sections. Each raises interesting questions for discussion. Part I is called "Ordinary Heroes." The young characters must decide whether to save themselves or another. Part II is called "Bad Luck or Bad Judgment?" and the unifying idea is that a "single decision can change your life forever." In Part III the stories explore the question of whether the risks heroes take are acts of madness or of courage. These ideas are interesting ones for students to think about not only in relation to literature but also in terms of their own lives.

• **Tomorrow When the War Began**

Tomorrow When the War Began is an exciting novel by Australian award winner, John Marsden and one of my own personal favorites. It has plenty of action and suspense as well as great characters who mature as they face life and death situations. It's very realistic – no happily-ever-after here.

Ellie and her friends go camping in the Australian bush for a week. When they return they find their homes deserted, their farm animals dead or dying. They soon discover that their families and all the families in the district are being held prisoner at the county showgrounds. Their country has been invaded by an unnamed army. In the space of a few hours, the safety they have known in their lives is shattered. The action speeds up, and the suspense never ends. I agree with one of my students who said, "I really like the *idea* of the book." Again, it's the idea of kids on their own against horrendous odds.

At first, they retreat back to the wilderness and try to decide what they should do. Surrender? Stay hidden and hope another nation comes to help? They choose to become guerrillas and fight against the enemy.

The cast of characters includes Ellie, the narrator and a strong, thoughtful leader, Lee, a quiet musician, Homer who's never seemed very serious but emerges as the real leader, and Fi who despite her delicacy and rather sheltered upbringing proves to be tough and brave. There are eight characters in all, and 7th grader, Betsy said that what she especially liked about this book was "how all the characters were different, but they all had personality traits that intertwined with each other to make really solid relationships among the characters. They all helped each other survive because they all kept each other going. I liked how the author not only made them get along really well, but put in conflicts, too, which made the story seem much more realistic." Indeed, the book is as much about relationships as it is about survival, and Marsden does an excellent job of balancing action-packed scenes with those in which he skillfully develops the characters and their relationships with each other.

There are many suspenseful scenes. Ellie drives a bucket loader down a city street at 3 a.m. to rescue Lee when he's shot in the leg and can't walk. She sets fire to a lawnmower that explodes and kills several enemy soldiers. She hides under a bed while a soldier is searching the room. They all escape from Corrie's house just before a plane flies over and bombs the house. They decide to blow up an important bridge, and Ellie drives a gas tanker under the bridge and sets it on fire.

The book ends without telling you what is going to happen. Corrie is badly shot, and Kevin is forced to drive her to the hospital, which is controlled by the enemy. Ellie, who keeps a journal, writes about the "loyalty, courage and goodness" of her friends. "We've got to stick together, that's all I know."

- **The Dead of Night**
- **A Killing Frost**
- **Darkness Be My Friend**
- **Burning for Revenge**

The good news is that Marsden ended the book that way so he could write a sequel. Actually, make that six sequels to date! If your students liked *Tomorrow When the War Began,* suggest they check out the following sequels: *The Dead of Night, A Killing Frost, Darkness Be My Friend, Burning for Revenge, The Night is For Hunting,* and *The Other Side of Dawn.* (As of this writing, the last two are only available in Australia.)

While I often find sequels to be disappointing compared to the original, Marsden's are just as intensely suspenseful as the original. I recently did a book group with twelve seventh graders, and it was clearly one of the most popular book groups I've ever done. For several months afterwards, students were eagerly passing around copies of the sequels.

Any one of these books would make for an exciting small group discussion. Another approach which worked well for me was to have each of my students read a different survival book. Because it is such a popular genre, many had previously read other survival novels as well. The variety of books stimulated a great deal of discussion. We tried to define a survival book, classify the ones we had read, and decide what the characters had learned from their ordeals.

Perhaps our most interesting talk focused on the qualities these characters had which enabled them to make it to the end of the book. One student began the discussion by observing that her character's intelligence helped him to stay alive. Others agreed that intelligence was important for their characters. When I probed for what they meant by intelligent, other thoughts emerged – an intelligent character can be flexible and adapt, think fast, learn fast, be inventive, and plan ahead, they said.

What else helped? I asked. Most agreed that being emotionally, as well as physically strong was important. One student explained, "My character had something to look forward to when the outlook seemed most bleak. She always kept a positive attitude." Someone added that his character had a goal. "A will to live kept my character going," said someone else. "She was determined and never gave up hope."

Another student felt his character survived because he was stubborn. "Mine survived because he was *not* stubborn, but could change and adapt," said another student. A third student volunteered that perhaps the ability to tell when to be stubborn and when not to be was the critical factor. We also discussed the difference between being stubborn and persevering. A similar discussion centered around taking risks to survive. We finally agreed that what was needed was good judgment to tell when to take risks and when to be cautious.

Thinking of others and being willing to sacrifice seemed important in a number of books. Working together helped save the character in others. In several books the support of friends and family was crucial. As one student added a characteristic to our growing list on the board, I'd see others nod in acknowledgment.

One student felt his character had many qualities that helped him to survive but that all those qualities wouldn't have helped if he had not also had luck. After a lengthy evaluation of the role of luck, students concluded that, while in most cases luck helped, it would not have been enough without the strengths of the characters.

Students like the action and the suspense created by the danger in survival stories. In addition, as one student articulated, it was not just seeing if the characters lived or died, because she was always pretty sure they would live, but she liked seeing how they coped with the obstacles. From the safety of their beds with the covers pulled securely up to their chins, students can imagine themselves in dangerous situations, without any adults to help, and, along with the character, they can test their own stamina. And as they read, they can ask themselves, "Do I have what it takes?" Good literature, and survival books in particular, leads to just this sort of reflection.

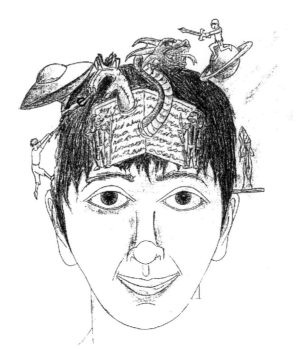

Drawing by Kyle Norris

When I open a book, all of a sudden I'm in the world of the characters. I become the main character and I'm living the story. I'm fighting the monster, I'm flying the space ship, and it's too hard to put the book down."
— Turner Carroll, Grade 8

PART II: THE OUTER WORLD

Books to help students develop understanding of and compassion for others

Reading is like looking at the world through the eyes of another person.—Caryn Devins, Grade 8

Chapter 4: Beyond Stereotypes
— Novels about growing up in other cultures —

Recently, my students and I were discussing the requirement that the President of the United States must be a natural born citizen. "I agree," said one girl. "We don't want someone who's come from China because they'd have a Chinese background. We want someone who's an American." I looked around the room and wondered, "Who do these kids think is an American?" There were some nods, and a few hands shot up to disagree. "It doesn't matter what their background is," argued a student. "As long as they were born here they have a right to run." Another boy jumped into the fray, "I think we should change the requirement. Their great-great grandparents should have been born in this country." **White. European**. The words hung unspoken in the classroom. Many students were nodding in agreement. In the front row, a girl who was born in Ghana sat expressionless. I wondered what she was feeling.

Essex is a suburban community of mostly middle class Whites, many of whom have moved here from other parts of the country to work at IBM. The University of Vermont, a half hour drive away, has recently been the center of considerable controversy over what some consider a lack of diversity in students, staff, and programs. Until quite recently, Vermont has attracted few families of non-European ancestry.

I've prided myself on exposing my students to other cultures through emphasis on current events, an annual International Festival project, and speakers from different countries throughout the year. But I was beginning to wonder whether it was enough. Perhaps there was a piece missing. Many students seemed to view people from backgrounds other than theirs as non-American, DIFFERENT, and, somehow, not worthy to lead the nation.

I was reminded of a passage from Hazel Rochman's book *Against Borders: Promoting Books for a Multicultural World:*

The best books break down borders. They surprise us - whether they are set close to home or abroad. They change our view of ourselves; they extend that phrase "like me" to include what we thought was foreign and strange...the real point of multicultural education: to help kids recognize their own culture and understand their connection with those who appear different.

...Books can make a difference in dispelling prejudice and building community...with enthralling stories that make us imagine the lives of others. A good story lets you know people as individuals in all their particularity and conflict; and once you see someone as a person – flawed, complex, striving – then you've reached beyond stereotypes.

The news stories we read and discuss, the guest speakers, the research on other countries, all bring other cultures into my classroom; but they don't show my students the heart and soul of another human being. Barring firsthand friendships, only good literature can do that.

Read Rochman's book if you have time. She has many useful lists of books centered around what she calls "mythic themes" such as the perilous journey, the hero and the monster, and outsiders. In addition to discussing books that fit these themes she also has extensive lists of books from different cultures.

I wanted to know which of the many multicultural books on the market today had the most "enthralling stories" to recommend to students. Which books would best help my students, with their limited view of the world, get to know someone from another culture as an individual with the same problems and fears?

Rochman warns in her book against making lists of such books and teaching them in isolation. She says that lists "function only as a well-meaning spotlight shining brightly but briefly on one cultural island or another, providing overdue recognition, yes, but imposing a different kind of isolation, celebratory but still separate." Her answer is to connect these books by including them in thematic studies. With this advice in mind, it may not be wise to simply teach a book in isolation or to have students read "books on different cultures."

As teachers we need to know the best multicultural books. If I'm studying Central America in social studies I may want to know which novels might supplement that study. If I'm doing a thematic study of families I might want to include a number of multicultural books. As I recommend good books to individual readers, I want to be sure that I'm not neglecting the many excellent books that are set in other cultures. Here then are some multicultural books to help begin to break down the barriers.

• Shabanu
• Haveli

Of all the books I've read that are set in other cultures, my favorite and the favorite of many of my students is *Shabanu* by Suzanne Fisher Staples. Shabanu's family are nomads in modern Pakistan in the desert region known as Cholistan. The book begins simply, immersing the reader in the everyday details of life – tending the camels, cooking chapatis over the open fire, getting water from the river. Suspense builds when Shabanu's family escapes in the night across the desert from a rich landlord who wants to steal Shabanu's sister Phulan. When Phulan's husband-to-be is killed, she is betrothed to the man Shabanu was going to marry, and Shabanu is promised to a 55-year-old man with three wives. Shabanu rebels against her father's choice and attempts to run away. When she finally returns ready to do her father's bidding, my students often argue fiercely against the injustice of it. But Staples has brought the Muslim world of the nomads so vividly to life that the ending is completely believable.

Shabanu is "struggling to know what it is to be grown." She is a feisty and brave character in a culture that does not value such traits in its females, and this creates conflicts. Her father, who attempts to raise his children in the traditional Muslim manner, is a man of intelligence and warmth whose love for his daughter transcends the expectations of society. Although Shabanu's life as a Muslim woman in a nomadic family is extremely different from that of an American adolescent, her conflicts with her father, her loss of a beloved animal, and her decision to defy the expectations of her society are all issues middle school readers can relate to. They may need some background on Muslim culture before beginning, and follow up discussions will certainly add to the depth of their understanding.

I have used this book with several different discussion groups. It has been one of the most successful discussion books I have used. Students invariably remember it fondly. "Oh, Shabanu," they say when it comes up later in conversation, "that was a wonderful book!" They always talk about Shabanu as though she's a close friend. I almost expect them to say, "I wonder what's become of her?"

Suzanne Fisher Staples must have wondered that, too, because she's written a sequel called *Haveli* about Shabanu's married life and which I would classify as an adult book. I have recommended it to only a handful of my most mature readers and instead urged those who loved *Shabanu* to save it for when they are a bit older.

TEACHING IDEA

Shabanu was one of a number of books I used for an evening discussion group of parents and children who read the book and then met to discuss it. Parents and students alike enjoyed the opportunity to share their ideas. One mother commented, "I loved reading the same book as my daughter. I liked seeing a different culture through her eyes." It was especially interesting for many of the parents and children to discuss role expectations of women in different cultures.

• Homeless Bird

In *Homeless Bird,* Gloria Whelan tells a simple story rich with cultural details of India. One of the things I especially like about this book is that its setting encompasses both rural and urban India. The reader learns about arranged marriages and wedding traditions, the sacredness of the Ganges River, funeral traditions, the conflict between traditional ways and the influence of western culture, and the habits of daily life. It would be interesting to compare the life of Koly in India with that of Shabanu in Pakistan.

The main character, Koly, is only 13 when her parents arrange a marriage for her. She soon finds herself married to Hari, a boy barely older than herself who is dying of tuberculosis. His parents had concealed this fact from Koly's parents so they could use her dowry money to take Hari to the sacred Ganges for a cure. With a deft hand and words that early middle grade readers can understand, Whelan paints a vivid picture of life along the Ganges:

Along the river's edge women were scrubbing clothes and even washing their pots and pans. Barbers were cutting hair. There were dogs and a cow wandering about. Two boys were flying kites. We saw people with every kind of illness. Some could not walk; others were as thin and wasted as Hari was; some had terrible sores and deformities. I could hardly bear to look at all the misery. Yet the expressions on the faces of the sick were not sad. They were not hopeful, but they were peaceful.

Unfortunately, Hari dies while at the Ganges, and just as suddenly as Koly found herself married, she now finds herself a widow.

According to tradition, she stays with Hari's family. Her mother-in-law is a bitter woman who not only constantly criticizes Koly's best efforts but also manages to cheat her out of her widow's pension. Koly's only pleasures are her friendship with Hari's sister, her love of embroidery, and the fact that her father-in-law is teaching her to read. When Hari's sister marries and moves away and her father-in-law dies, Koly's life looks bleak indeed.

Her life takes a dramatic turn when her mother-in-law abandons her in the holy city of Vrindavan, a city of widows. Koly is frightened at being alone in a large city with nowhere to go and for a few days she lives and sleeps on the streets. Raji, a rickshaw boy, takes pity on her and takes her to a home for young widows. Here Maa Kamala helps her find a job stringing marigold garlands.

Whelan gives the reader a flavor of life in the city in this passage as Koly and a friend hurry to work:

We had to pick our way over sleeping bodies. Whole households of baaps, maas, and children lay on their charpoys or on the sidewalk. On the way to the bazaar we passed the doorway where I had spent my nights. Another widow was curled up there, still asleep...

Whelan also brings alive the sights and sounds and smells of a busy city street – booths of brightly colored cloth, cars, and rickshaws, and cows vying for space, and the rich scent of heaps of spices at the open stalls.

Life gets even better for Koly when the rich woman who owns the widow's house discovers her great skill at embroidery. She finds her a job with a maker of fine saris where she meets other girls like herself and gains even more skill at embroidery.

Meanwhile, her friendship with Raji blossoms and when he finally asks her to marry him and move to his village in the countryside, Koly is torn between her love of her work in the city and her love for Raji. But this is definitely a happily-ever-after kind of book. Raji builds a special room onto his new house for Koly's embroidery workshop and her boss allows her to sew at home and bring her work into the city to him each month.

This is an excellent book to introduce middle grade readers to India and to a likeable young girl with the strength to make a life for herself within the traditions of her culture.

• Against the Storm

Against the Storm, by Gaye Hiçyilmaz is another of the best multicultural books. Set in Turkey, it is, like *Shabanu,* a coming of age story. Mehmet's family moves from the small village where he has lived all his life to Ankara where they believe that, like Mehmet's uncle Yusuf, they can have a better life. But they end up in an unfinished apartment in a shanty town with Mehmet's father sweeping floors in Yusuf's shop. Hiçyilmaz shows many contrasts between the haves and the have nots in this Turkish city. The contrast between a relatively self-sufficient life in a rural area and the difficulties of surviving in the city is also strongly depicted.

When his young cousin dies because the family wouldn't take her to the hospital, Mehmet is enraged by their passivity. "They knew how to die. They knew a million ways to die, but they did not know how to live." As the other members of the family fail to stand up to Uncle Yusuf's cruel treatment of them, Mehmet becomes more distant from them. He gets a job collecting fares on a minibus and spends more and more time with his friend Muhlis, a streetwise orphan who is a warm, endearing character.

Mehmet has another friend, Hayri, who, like Mehmet's own family, believes that although the present looks bleak, "there's not much we can do about it, is there? We can't change things, can we?" But Mehmet believes he *can* change things, *can* make his life better. As he grows stronger and more independent, he and Muhlis decide to leave Ankara and go back to Mehmet's village and start a new life. Then, in an unexpected scene, during a storm, Muhlis, because he doesn't know any better, touches a downed electrical wire, is electrocuted and dies. Another death. Ignorance. Poverty. A vicious cycle from which Mehmet is more determined than ever to escape.

With a small gift of money from a rich woman to help him get started, he sets off alone to return to his village. Is it luck or determination that enables people to begin a new life, to escape from destructive cycles? This would be an excellent question to debate with students before and after they read this book.

Although Uncle Yusuf and his son are portrayed as too uncaring, and although the way Mehmet reacts to Muhlis's death doesn't quite ring true, the book has much going for it that overshadows these problems. The action moves along at a good rate with just enough suspense to hold students' interest. Mehmet is a likable character whom you find yourself rooting for, and the secondary characters of Muhlis, Mehmet's sister, Ayse, his dog, Korsan, and the rich elderly woman who befriends him are all well drawn. In addition to learning about life in Turkey, children who live so comfortably can see what it's like to live on the edge of survival. A sixth grade girl who described this book as "really powerful" wrote, "The hardship that Mehmet went through made me want to give him all the money I had! The way his family just didn't care enraged me! The book really hooked me because I almost felt like somehow Mehmet would be safe if I kept reading."

• A Thief in the Village and Other Stories of Jamaica

A Thief in the Village and Other Stories of Jamaica by James Berry has wonderful short stories for reading aloud. The stories are rich with the details of ordinary life, strong emotions, and moments of clear insight. Some of the stories are about the longings of children. In "Becky and the Wheel-and-Brake Boys," Becky dreams day and night of a bike despite her grandmother's dire warnings of tomboys coming to bad ends.

In "Fanso and Granny-Flo" Fanso longs to get to know his father who suddenly appears out of nowhere after deserting his mother before he was born. His mother and grandmother are determined to keep him away from the man. Students will sympathize with Fanso's explosion of feelings at seeing his father for a few minutes only to have him disappear again.

Other stories are about being different and the cruelties people of all ages can inflict on those who look or act different. In "Elias and the Mongoose," one of the most striking stories, a disabled boy is continually tortured by the other boys. In a horrible scene they incite a dog to attack him as he tries to protect his pet mongoose from them. His grandmother comes home just in time to catch the boys and they are punished. But the story ends with these words, "The dust of the trouble settled. The boys began to reexamine their mistake. They decided it was all bad luck that Granny returned when she did. They began plotting again about how to get the mongoose without getting a beating." It would be interesting to read only as far as the attack, let students write their own endings, and then compare theirs to Berry's.

Reading these stories aloud will evoke the culture of Jamaica, and Berry's poetic language will roll off your tongue. Becky, Fanso, Elias, indeed all of Berry's characters are people your students will feel close to. They will understand their feelings and wish their acquaintance were not so brief.

• Join In

Another very interesting collection of stories is *Join In.* Donald R. Gallo has collected and edited these multi-ethnic short stories. In the introduction, Gallo writes, "The destructive Los Angeles race riots in the spring of 1992 and the murderous attempts at "ethnic cleansing" currently taking place in various parts of the world are striking evidence of the need for tolerance and understanding of the difference among us…Can we stop hating each other? Can we stop fighting with each other? Can we start understanding one another? It is my hope, and the hope of the authors represented here, that this collection of short stories might help just a little toward that end."

Most of the authors are Black, Asian, and Latino. Some are Caucasians who have known or worked with people from other races. After each story, a nice touch is that Gallo includes information about the author's background, other writings, and where the idea for the story came from.

The characters in these stories are Vietnamese, Lebanese, Laotian, Cuban, Cambodian, Pueblo Indian, Puerto Rican, Chinese, Japanese, and Black. They all live in the United States. Some are recent immigrants; others are second or third generation Americans. All are teenagers grappling with issues of fitting in, making friends, facing prejudice, and discovering their true identity. All of the stories are interesting and you can find your own favorites that you think would appeal to your students. Some of my favorites, which make great read-alouds and lead to stimulating class discussions are "Eagle Cloud and Fawn," "No Win Phuong," and "The Winter Hibiscus."

"Eagle Cloud and Fawn" by Barbara Beasley Murphy is a simple story of the beginning of a friendship between a Pueblo boy and an Anglo girl. Paul, a Pueblo, picks up an Anglo girl at the hotel where he works as a waiter. He's hardly ever talked to an non-Indian girl before, but he's attracted to Fawn who is traveling alone. As they share their feelings and dreams with each other, barriers that exist between a Native American and the White world are broken. This is just one individual getting to know another. They are fascinated by their differences. Paul takes her to visit Tesuque pueblo and explains his role as an antelope dancer in their celebrations. But the similarities overshadow the differences and cement the friendship. When Fawn tells Paul about the death of her beloved grandfather, Paul realizes that he feels "sorry for an Anglo for the first time." There are subtle clues that this will not be an easy friendship to maintain. Paul is unsure if his family will accept an Anglo. Students will be interested in discussing what they think will happen to Paul and Fawn's relationship.

"No Win Phuong" by Alden R. Carter is also about friendship and one boy's persistence in trying to understand a new boy who's Vietnamese. Bull is willing to take a risk and reach out to Phuong, willing to learn from him when he unknowingly says something racist and Phuong points it out, and willing to work patiently with Phuong to help him become an exceptional pitcher.

Although Phuong has excellent pitching skills, he falls apart in a real game because he cares too much about winning. He says, "I'd love to be part of a team, but nobody ever puts up with me very long...so I go my own way." Bull works with Phuong day after day, slowly increasing his confidence and his concentration.

The prejudice in this story may be subtle for some middle grade readers. For example, Bull's friend, Jeff, says when he first meets Phuong, "I thought all Vietnamese were short." As you read the story aloud you could ask students to identify the generalizations about Vietnamese that the characters make. An interesting question for discussion would be "Who is the hero of this story?" Is it Bull who teaches Phuong or Phuong who learns from Bull? Are they equally heroes?"

"The Winter Hibiscus" by Minfong Ho (see Chapter 5 for the Ho novel, *The Clay Marble*) is my favorite story in this collection. Saeng is a Laotian immigrant who is about to take her driver's test. A rite of passage for any teenager, passing the test is even more important for Saeng. Her family has finally scraped together enough money for a car and they need her to drive them to work to save time and bus fares.

Saeng is borrowing their sponsor's son's car. Although Saeng is attracted to the son, David, she knows that he is nice to her only because of his mother. Saeng gets nervous during the driving test and fails. This seems to symbolize her failure to fit into her new world, and she is overcome by despair. On her way home, she is drawn to a greenhouse and in the moist shelter of the familiar tropical plants she remembers her home and her grandmother. "A wave of loss so deep and strong that it stung Saeng's eyes now swept over her…A blink, a channel switch, a boat ride in the night, and it was all gone. Irretrievably, irrevocably gone." This would be a good story for students to practice reading between the lines to find the meaning. The meaning is revealed near the end when Saeng buys a hibiscus plant as a memory of home. As she plants it, she realizes that it is important to remember the past but also to adapt to the present. Almost reluctantly, she realizes that many of the things she had "thought of as strange before had become, through the quiet repetition of season upon season, almost familiar to her now." Lifted out of despair, she resolves to take the driver's test again in the spring.

There are many other excellent stories in this collection. Linda Crew (see *Children of the River* in Chapter 5) writes "Bride Price," a story about a Cambodian girl and the conflict she feels between fitting into the American teen culture and following the ways of the Cambodian culture.

"Dead End" by Rudolfo Annya is about the dilemma faced by a studious young Hispanic when one of the most popular boys in school tries to seduce her away from her goals. Should she give in to his sweet kisses and his offer of sweet smoke and join the gang, or should she continue to be different and pursue her dream of a good education. "Dead End" has a similar theme to *True Believer* in Chapter 6 and would be a good story to pair with the novel.

"Rima's Song" by Elsa Marston is about a group of young musicians and the arrival of a cousin from Lebanon. The sight of blood stirs up memories of the war zone he left behind.

In "A Daughter of the Sea" by Maureen Wartski, Lien faces the indifference and hostility of her classmates toward Asians. On a biology field trip, when Lien and a group of other students work hard to save a beached whale, they begin to see each other as individuals.

Many of the stories in this collection seem to suggest that the way to break the stereotypes that exist is through individuals and small groups getting to know each other.

• For the Life of Laetitia

Merle Hodge's *For the Life of Laetitia* is set in an unspecified Caribbean country, perhaps the author's native Trinidad. As the book opens, Laetitia leaves her tightly-knit, extended family and travels to the city to live with the father she barely knows so she can attend secondary school. Although determined to get an education, Laetitia struggles to adjust to her new life. Her father is a cruel man and the danger of abuse is always there, subtly menacing.

At first, Laetitia does well in school. Middle school readers will be able to relate to her lively account of students and mixed review of their teachers. She becomes friends with Anjanee who lives in a rural area. Because she must get up at 4 a.m. to do her household work and then travel by foot and bus to reach the city school, Anjanee often falls asleep in class. Although her family doesn't see any need for a girl to get an education, Anjanee works hard to succeed and make a better life for herself and her mother.

When her father won't let her go home on the weekends, Laetitia rebels – cutting classes, failing tests, and breaking school rules. Then Anjanee commits suicide, and Laetitia ends up in the hospital with a nervous breakdown. She recovers and returns to her family, determined to never again live with her father and to continue her schooling despite the difficulties of getting there from her rural home.

Laetitia tells the story in a voice rich with the rhythms of her people, and this may prove a bit difficult for some readers. The plot moves slowly, but it is a rich story well worth the effort of your better readers. Two eighth grade girls who read it both enjoyed it very much. They said it read like non-fiction, and they enjoyed learning about life in another culture. One said, "You learn about everything from the food, to the schools, to the racial prejudices people have. I liked being able to sit back and imagine what it would be like to live in a place like that."

• Among the Volcanoes

In *Among the Volcanoes,* by Omar S. Castaneda, Isabel lives in a remote Mayan village in Guatemala. Her dream of becoming a teacher is thwarted when her mother, Manuela, becomes dangerously ill, and Isabel must quit school to care for her. She is torn between her desire to pursue her own goals and wanting to help her family.

Allan Waters, a young American medical researcher, comes to the village and says that he can help her mother. But the villagers, who rely on traditional healing methods, fear and mistrust him. Isabel thinks he may be able to help, but her father explains, "Anything new is very dangerous, Isabel. People are afraid. You're still so young. You don't know. Something that can seem innocent can hold a terrible poison. That's the way it is here. The poor have no possibility of changing anything..." But like Mehmet in *Against the Storm*, Isabel believes in the possibility of change.

When the mother's condition worsens, Allan Waters convinces the family to go to a hospital in the nearest city. The scene at the hospital is well done, vividly showing how scared both Isabel and her mother are of the doctor's stethoscope. The doctor says Manuela needs tests and treatment, but she refuses these and returns to her village. Isabel realizes her mother will soon die and with her, Isabel's own dreams will also die.

In what is the weakest part of the book, Isabel turns to her teacher for advice. In a long, didactic passage he tells her "You can be different...You don't have to do what everyone else says. It won't be easy for you, but you don't have to kill your hopes." Isabel realizes that she wants to stay in her village and marry Lucas, but she also wants to be a teacher. She talks forthrightly to Lucas and convinces him to help her reach her goal. We know it won't be easy and we're not sure she'll succeed but we finish the book knowing that Isabel and Lucas will do their best to forge a new lifestyle without completely giving up the traditional ways.

There is one graphic scene where guerrillas kill a villager's steer as Isabel watches from a hiding place. There are also a couple of instances of strong language, which while appropriate to the story, might offend younger readers.

The book does an excellent job of showing the conflict between change and tradition, conflict that is occurring in so many parts of the world today as western ways spread rapidly throughout the developing world. Although Isabel's world is so different from ours, she is like all of us - needing to find her place in the world and to find the courage to be herself even though what she wants is different from what her family and society expect.

Lauren, a sixth grader who really liked this book, wrote, "I think the moral of this story is to hold onto your dreams and keep them alive. I've learned a lot about Guatemalan life from this book and hope I can read another just as good as this one."

• Taste of Salt

Taste of Salt, by the late Frances Temple is a powerful portrait of life in modern Haiti. As the novel opens in 1991, Aristide has just been elected President of Haiti. Djo, a seventeen year old follower of Aristide, is in the hospital on the verge of death from a firebombing and beating by the Tonton Macoutes, a private army of thugs.

Jeremie, a young girl raised in a convent, has been sent by Aristide to tape Djo's life story. She, too, eventually tells her story, and although her life has been quite different from Djo's life on the streets and in the shelter Aristide has set up for homeless boys, she, too has been influenced by Aristide.

This is also Aristide's story, and the strands of history and modern politics are seamlessly woven into the story and never allowed to overshadow the characters and the story of their lives. Perhaps even more, it is Haiti's story. I learned a lot about Haiti myself from this book and highly recommend it to adults as well as students. Students who read it for a book discussion with me loved the book and had a heated debate about who was the main character. Some argued passionately for Haiti as the main character while others maintained that Djo and Jeremie shared that honor. They were shocked by the images of poverty and thrilled that Djo and Jeremie were fighting to make a better life for themselves and their people.

There is plenty of action and suspense for adolescent readers. At 13 Djo is kidnapped and forced to work on a sugar cane plantation in the Dominican Republic. He plots his escape and finally returns to Port au Prince to fight against the military dictatorship. There are narrow escapes from raids by the Macoutes, and Djo's best friend dies in one of the attacks. Jeremie defies her mother and the nuns as she becomes increasingly drawn into the democratic movement. She is present at Ruelle Vaillant when voters are gunned down. "A responsible person in Haiti cannot stay far from trouble," she says.

The voices and personalities of Djo and Jeremie, as they tell their respective stories, draw students into their lives and their world. Like Djo and Jeremie, the reader, too, will cling to the hope for a better tomorrow for Haitian people.

For younger readers, Temple's *Tonight by Sea* gives a good picture of life in Haiti. See Chapter 5 for a discussion of this book.

• Go and Come Back

It's always interesting and informative to look at another culture and observe both the differences and the similarities. Joan Abelove, in *Go and Come Back,* takes the young adult cultural novel a step further and forces American readers to look at their own culture with new eyes. The novel is set in the Amazonian jungle of Peru along the eastern slopes of the Andes where the Isabos live much as their ancestors have for centuries, virtually untouched by the modern world. The author, who has a doctorate in cultural anthropology, lived for two years among people much like the characters in the novel, but out of respect for them has changed the name of the village and the ethnic group. The story is told through the eyes of Alicia, a young Isabo who studies the two anthropologists just as keenly as they study her and the life of the village. At first, Alicia is disgusted by the endless questions they ask, their complete lack of knowledge about how to live, and particularly by what she sees as their stinginess. But soon her own curiosity gets the best of her and she decides it is up to her to teach these two helpless women.

Alicia's mother sees the two women as trouble, as "different from real people…They only like their own kind. They will never like us. That is why I say they are trouble. Because you can never be sure what they are thinking, what they might do. They have no love of us, no appreciation of us…They are not the real people." Alicia, however, is more of a thinker than her mother. "Life was simple for my mother. She knew everything there was to know. Our caibo [people] are good, all others are bad. And that was all there was in the world." Alicia is getting used to the two women and no longer sees them as strangers. She likes listening to their music and learning about their lives back in New York City.

In the meantime, the reader learns, along with the two women, about life in the Amazon jungle – the food, the daily chores, the roles of men and women, the sexual practices. Alicia adopts a young Spanish baby whose father was threatening to kill it and raises it as her own. The rhythm of daily life goes on. "The gnats came out in the morning, the mosquitoes when the sun set. Some good things happened, some bad. Cornelia's baby was born. Philiberto's baby died. Metza Shoko cured Amalia's stomachache. Yamiquenti still didn't get pregnant. Elena's younger brother Nelson had sex for the first time…Boshi brought me yellow and red thread from Tarapoto and went off to work wood upriver with Jose Elenario."

The pace of the book is slow and the writing spare and elegant. It is not a book that all students will like. But for those who have the patience to read it, it will bring its own rewards. In the end as a plane arrives to take the two women away after their year's stay in the village, one of the women invites Alicia to take a short ride. Alicia bravely accepts and from the air she sees the village and the expanse of jungle beyond it and beyond that the mountains. "…now I could see the big river, with our little river flowing into it. And I could see all the little streams that fed our little river. Then we were coming down to our river again, right on top of it. The plane stopped and we were back in my old world and it looked the same as when we left it, but now I knew that it also looked different when you looked at it from another view." Good literature has the power to give the reader not just a view of the unknown world but a different perspective on his own world as well.

• Broken Bridge

Broken Bridge by Lynne Reid Banks is set in modern Israel. Banks is one of the few authors I know of who writes about the conflicts in Israel in fiction making them accessible to young adults. Although I have some problems with the resulting book, there are many things about it to like. First, of importance for the raised-on-TV generation, there's suspense. Nili who lives on a kibbutz, and her visiting Canadian cousin, Glen, are attacked by two Arabs as they walk down the street in Jerusalem. Glen is killed and Nili miraculously escapes death, thanks to one of the Arabs who decides at the last minute to save her. Then there is the search for the men who attacked them, told from the men's viewpoint in hiding and from the views of the members of the kibbutz, especially Glen's father, who desperately wants to confront his son's murderer.

Second, although Banks is clearly interested in informing her readers about the history and current affairs of Israel, she goes beyond that to take us into the hearts of her large cast of characters. There is Nili who holds her guilt inside when faced with the police line-up of suspects; she chooses not to identify the man who saved her life. There is Yoni, her cousin, who tries to reconcile his duty as a soldier in the Israeli army with his guilt for breaking the arms of young Arabs during the Intifada. Nili's brother, Nimrod, wrestles with what it means to be a man and with his anger at Nili for not identifying the man who could lead them to Glen's killer. Banks reveals the inner lives of her adult characters as well – Glen's father who is dealing with his own guilt for having left Israel years ago, Nili's grandfather, Nat, who continues to fight for peace with the Arabs despite losing his grandson, and Nili's mother who continues her work to achieve justice for Arabs.

Banks tries to portray all sides of the conflict, but it is clear that she is in favor of making peace with the Arabs and turning over the West Bank and Gaza to them. As Nat tells a militant high school student, "Think, think! Use your imaginations! In destroying them, we destroy ourselves! They are like us! No worse, no better!"

Banks gives us a brief look into the lives of the Arabs who attacked Nili and Glen as they hide from the police and finally as one tries to escape to Jordan. She tries to show the reader the humanity of these men. As Yoni says, "It doesn't take much to turn a man into something different than he might have been. Injustice and pain, and especially fear, can change people very quickly. That's why you have to be so careful how you treat people."

• One More River

One of the concerns I have with this book is that the plot is built on the idea that the Arab who saved Nili's life is the same man her mother befriended 25 years ago in the prequel to this book, *One More River,* the story of Israel a generation earlier. I find this coincidence difficult to accept and because it's a recurring thread in the story, I kept finding myself annoyed with the contrivance.

My other criticism is that there are too many characters with too many problems, and too many of those characters are adults. I think Banks would have had a more concise and powerful story if she hadn't tried to do so much. However, we desperately need books on the Middle East for young adult readers, and *Broken Bridge,* despite its problems, has a lot going for it. The many issues Banks explores will lead to lively debates and help students see that there are many positions on any conflict. An acquaintance with Nili and her family and friends will give a new dimension to the conflict in Israel as well as help students see that both Israelis and Arabs are, indeed, "like us."

• Habibi

Habibi by Naomi Shihab Nye is a poignant coming-of-age story with the same message. It is a more straightforward story than *Broken Bridge* with a less complex plot, but Nye's rich language will appeal to your more sophisticated readers. Liyana Abboud is 14 when her family decides to move to Israel where her father was born. Liyana's father is Arabic, her mother is American, and, until now, she has not thought too much about who she is. In Jerusalem her world with all its familiar details is gone and it's like beginning her life anew. "No one really knew her here, no one knew what she liked, or who her friends had been, or how funny she could be…She would have to start from scratch…"

Luckily, Liyana is bright and resourceful, and she makes the adjustment more easily than many would. However, she is sometimes disconcerted at the different values she encounters. Her father's elder brother asks for her hand in marriage to his son. She hears that an Arab boy was beaten up for kissing a girl. Her father tells her that you can't "measure one country's customs by another's," and Liyana laments that "With her luck she had been born into the only non-kissing culture, just when it started feeling like a valuable activity."

Liyana spends weekends in the West Bank village with her large extended family getting to know her grandmother. During the week she lives in Jerusalem and attends an Armenian private school where she is the only non-Armenian.

Liyana runs head on into the Jewish-Palestinian conflict when she meets Omer, a Jewish boy to whom she is immediately attracted. Their friendship is not easy in Jerusalem where "so much old anger floated around, echoed from fading graffiti, seeped out of cracks. Sometimes it bumped into new anger in the streets. The air felt stacked with weeping and raging and praying to God by all the different names." As the story progresses, Nye writes tenderly of Liyana's and Omer's deepening feelings for each other.

Nye also skillfully weaves in details about the conflict. Liyana and her brother become friends with two children who live in a Palestinian refugee camp next to their apartment and learn how their village was taken away by Israeli soldiers. When she shops in a spice shop run by an Arab, a Jewish man tells her, "Why bother with this animal?...Go to better stores in our part of town." As one student who loved this book said, "I think this book is perfect for anyone who wants to learn about the Middle East without reading a boring textbook."

For many chapters, daily life slowly unfolds as Nye describes it in her sparse but poetic style. Then suddenly, the routine explodes in a moment of violence. A bomb in a Jewish market place leads to soldiers coming to the refugee camp and shooting at their friend, Kahled. Poppy gets involved and winds up in jail. Liyana bravely goes to visit him in jail and stands up to the soldiers. "YOU DO NOT HAVE TO BE THIS WAY!" she tells them defiantly.

Liyana, like the students who walk through your classroom door each day, is subtly molding herself into the adult she will become. She's choosing what to value. After seeing live chickens imprisoned in cages in the butcher shop she decides to become a vegetarian. She examines her parents' values, keeping some, discarding others. She challenges her parents when they don't want to take Omer to visit the Palestinian village where their extended family lives. Poppy argues, "They wouldn't – understand. It would seem suspicious – or unsettling to them. The peace isn't stabilized enough yet." But Liyana challenges this, "What good is it to believe in peace and talk about peace if you only want to live the same old ways?...We want to write a new story."

Poppy finally agrees to take Omer and Liyana and her brother's Palestinian friends to visit the family. Sitti, Liyana's wise grandmother, sums up the theme of this book when she says, "You will need to be brave. There are hard days coming. There are hard words waiting in people's mouths to be spoken. There are walls. You can't break them. Just find doors in them. See...You already have. Here we are, together." We live in a world where walls are far too common. *Habibi* helps the young adult reader to see the possibility of doors. It's a book that will linger in your memory, in your heart.

• AK

AK, by Peter Dickinson, is set in modern Africa in a fictionalized country and is as current as today's headlines. Michael Nagomi, the leader of a commando unit, adopts Paul, a young boy who has been orphaned by the war. He teaches him how to be a warrior and gives him an AK47. When the war ends, Michael gets a job in the new government that faces the challenges of corruption in its own ranks, conflicts between rival gangs and political groups, and widespread poverty with its accompanying hopelessness.

The leader of the new government is soon assassinated, and Michael is imprisoned. His son Paul is also in danger, and he and his friends escape from boarding school and head toward the capitol to rescue Michael.

One of Dickinson's purposes seems to be to explore how a fractured nation with so many problems can pull itself together to become a strong and viable country. He believes that a big part of the answer lies in the strength of the people themselves. He sees the craftsmen and entrepreneurs as the lifeblood of the new nation and creates a strong woman character to organize them to march on the palace and demand their rights. At the same time, Paul gets people organized to demand freedom for Michael.

Matt is a student who rated *AK* highly. He wrote: "I think this book is an excellent combination of information and a good plot to get an important point across. It is much more interesting than a totally non-fiction piece that just states an opinion and backs it up with facts. I think the theme of this book is that Africans have to unite and be willing to fight even in the face of adversity to break the powerful grip of war in their countries."

Dickinson ends the book by giving the reader a choice between two completely different endings, both twenty years in the future. In one, the fighting has stopped and the country is slowly prospering. In the more pessimistic ending, the war rages on and on, and Paul is shot by one of his own guerrillas while he's on a mission. A group of my students who read this book had a lively debate about which ending was the most realistic.

This is not an easy book, and some students who chose it because they liked the cover that depicts Paul with his AK47 were disappointed. But for your more mature readers, it is excellent. It has a lot to teach the reader about life in Africa, the complexity of politics, and the power a group of people can have to make positive changes.

JP is an eighth grade reader who reads adult fiction almost exclusively. He said of *AK*, "It's the best young adult book I've read in a long time." JP is a serious writer and he admired the author's style. He wrote in his journal, "Wow! 'A few women and children, listless with heat, moved about, but the men lay like dead bodies in any shade they could find.' I can just picture it and it's not a pretty sight. The feeling of desolation just seems to ooze out of this book and the plot continues to thicken. The author really does a good job of portraying an unstable government. I can't wait to see what's next."

When he had finished the book he wrote, "I don't think I've ever read a book with a more climactic and satisfying end. From the huge gang war to the titanic riot, the last third of *AK* was intense. The details in the riot scene were great. The author really managed to conjure up the image of a mob stretching into the distance...Too bad there's no sequel."

• Chain of Fire

Another book set in Africa is *Chain of Fire* by Beverley Naidoo. The story begins when Naledi and her family discover that their South African village has been targeted for removal to the "homelands" and unfolds over the course of several weeks as the villagers seek to make their feelings known to the government. Charlotte, a sixth grader who read this book during our study of Africa, reacted strongly to the beginning of the book. "If I was one of those people who was living in that village at that time I would be so angry and hurt. I can't imagine what it would be like being forced out of my home without my permission...I don't know yet, but the village sounds tough especially Naledi. She sounds like she is ready to definitely fight back."

Charlotte's prediction is correct. The children stage a peaceful protest march, but the police attack them with dogs and whips. As crisis follows crisis, the violence builds, and Naledi and her brother become more deeply involved in the struggle. Their peaceful resistance reminded Jonathan of Ghandi's protests in India. He especially liked the quote, "As the van bumped noisily along the track, it seemed to Naledi that they were not continually at the edge of a sharp blade. The authorities were chopping at them from all sides, and yet, they were managing to hold on to the threads of life." Jonathan wrote in his log that this quote "shows how strong the people are and how they stick together no matter how big the struggle.

And every time the government tries to tear them apart, they just get stronger."

Later in his log, Jonathan writes, "To relate to what we were learning in class [about the history of Africa during the colonial period], in the book the White people just order around the Africans, not worrying about their lives and what that would do to them. A lot of people in the book will have a very hard time if the White people make the Africans move. This just shows how the White government's rule was so cruel in some places in Africa."

The awesome power of the Apartheid government rolls over them, and they watch as a huge bulldozer plows down their houses and crops. They are forced to move to an arid piece of land filled with row upon row of stifling tin shanties. Naledi and the other villagers vow to continue their fight.

The characters are well drawn and the action quickly paced. A group of students who read the book were fascinated by this piece of South African history and glad that Apartheid has been abolished despite the difficulties that remain for achieving racial harmony and justice. Bobby, who loved this book, said, "I especially liked how they kept fighting and never gave up." He was inspired by the book to write a story of his own set in South Africa.

TEACHING IDEA

Hazel Rochman has written an excellent collection of stories about South Africa called *Somehow Tenderness Survives*. Some of the stories have some sexual content that might be appropriate only for more mature readers. However, there are several that would be good to read aloud. I especially liked "Crackling Day" by Peter Abrahams and "A Day in the Country" by Dan Jacobson.

• A Girl Named Disaster

A Girl Named Disaster by Nancy Farmer is also set in Africa. It takes place in Mozambique and Zimbabwe and is a book that my sixth, seventh, and eighth graders enjoyed equally in a recent book group I led. However, at 300 pages, it is best for students who love to read.

There is a wealth of information about the Shona culture and about the land and the animals, but it is far more than this. It is the coming-of-age story of 11-year-old Nhamo who, fleeing an arranged marriage to a cruel man, sets out alone on the Musengezi River to find her father in Zimbabwe. It is also the exciting story of her survival story on the journey as she struggles against starvation, wild animals, the dangers of navigating the river in a leaky boat, and her own loneliness. "…one morning the lonely-sickness struck her with such force, her spirit felt like it was being circled by hyenas." Alison, a sixth grader, wondered what she would have done in Nhamo's place. "I don't know if I would have tried to go to Zimbabwe alone. Nhamo can't swim, is terrified of crocodiles, doesn't know how to paddle the boat, and doesn't even know where Zimbabwe is. She is a very brave girl. She is much braver than I am!"

Several times during the journey Nhamo is in danger of starving. At other times she is in danger from hippos and baboons. It is only due to her own cleverness at solving problems and her strong spirit that she survives. Most of my students who read this book seemed to think that some of the survival scenes were too long. They were especially frustrated with the length of time Nhamo spends on the baboon island and felt there were simply too many disasters in her life.

Nhamo also has some help surviving from the spirit world, and her frequent conversations with her dead mother and other spirits help her keep going. An interesting addition to the plot is the traditional stories that Nhamo tells to the spirits to stave off loneliness. During a group discussion, students wondered if Farmer had included the stories for another reason. After examining a number of stories they concluded that the stories have morals that Nhamo needs to keep going. For example, in several stories the underdog wins, and students felt that Nhamo, the outcast and underdog, would be inspired by this message.

When Nhamo at last reaches civilization she faces a whole new set of challenges. For awhile she stays at a scientific community and feels that she belongs. Then she discovers that her father has died and is taken to live with her father's family where she is treated as an outcast by everyone but her great-grandfather. But she is going to school and loves it. She maintains contact with her "family" at the scientific center and spends her summer vacations there. We don't know what will become of her, but we know she is a bold, independent young woman, and we could easily predict that she will forge a good life for herself.

TEACHING IDEA

Each year our team studies a different part of the world and holds an international festival. During our 1999 study of Africa students learned about the history, geography, and culture of Africa through reading non-fiction. Each student also read a novel set in Africa and participated in a series of discussions led by an adult volunteer.

For this type of project I needed books with a variety of reading levels as well as ones that would appeal to both boys and girls. I used: *A Girl Named Disaster,* by Nancy Farmer (see summary above); *Thunder Cave,* by Roland Smith. This fast-paced adventure story appealed to many of my students. The reading is easy, and Smith spins an interesting tale of an American boy who goes to Kenya in search of his father and is helped on his quest by a Masai. Smith weaves in issues of the extinction of elephants and the impact of drought on Africa; *AK,* by Peter Dickinson (see summary above); *Chain of Fire,* by Beverley Naidoo (see summary above); and *The Captive,* by Joyce Hansen. In this easy historical fiction, an African boy is kidnapped and sold into slavery. He ends up in the American colonies in Massachusetts and begins a life as a boat builder. Eventually, he sails to Africa to help his countrymen.

In each of these engaging books, readers will encounter a variety of characters dealing with different complex emotions. They'll find stories of friendship, family conflict, survival, and love. Your adolescent readers will discover that, although the details of these characters' lives are different, they have much in common. In their hearts they are alike.

Drawing by Emily Herder

The best job in the world would be reading good books all day long.
— Annica Crouse, Grade 8

Reading gives me a window into other lives, struggles, and times.
— Maggie Satink, Grade 7

Chapter 5: No Longer Strangers
— *Novels about refugees* —

Imagine yourself leaving home in the middle of the night with only the belongings you can carry. You leave stealthily, silently, the fear of discovery a terrifying presence blocking out all other thoughts. Only later does it hit you that you may never return. Your friends, your precious family photos, the big chair you curl up in to read are all left behind. After a long and desperate journey you arrive in an overcrowded camp where there is little privacy. Disease and danger are everywhere. You survive each difficult day with a flicker of hope that someday, somehow you'll be able to travel to a new country and start a new life.

For some 18 million people who live as refugees and another 23 to 40 million who are displaced persons in their own countries, this is the reality of their lives. Hardly a small number! Yet except for images on our TV screen of strangers in far away places – families desperately fleeing Kosovo, starving refugees in Africa, Kurdish refugees huddled together in a camp, Bosnian Muslims being herded onto a bus – we seldom think of these people. Most of our students know little, if anything, about them. Despite the problems many of our students face in their own families, the vast majority have a physical place to call home, a place of warmth and shelter with a daily meal.

Reading about the lives of young refugees helps students to imagine the lives of people whose experiences are so different from theirs. Middle school students with their strong sense of justice are intrigued to learn that so many people their own age are without homes or homelands. In addition, within their lifetime, the world community will most likely be forced to deal with the refugee situation in some way. As nationalistic fervor flares across the globe, the problems continue to grow, and more people are displaced each day. Famine and drought, war and politics, ethnic and religious hatred – all contribute to the growing number of displaced persons.

When I began to investigate young adult fiction about refugees, I was pleased by the number of good books available. I discovered, too, that the books are far more than a "lesson" on refugees and history. Most share two themes. One is that families and friends are invaluable in supporting each other through the most inhumane situations. The other is that each individual has the ability to find within himself an untapped strength to deal with the most unimaginable events and circumstances.

Here are some of the best books I found.

• Tonight by Sea
• Grab Hands and Run

Two of the most interesting books by the late Frances Temple are about journeys of escape from repressive governments. Both books can be read by a majority of middle school readers, and both have enough suspense to capture students' interest.

In *Tonight by Sea,* Temple deftly evokes life in Belle Fleuve, a small Haitian village by the sea. Paulie and her friend Karyl play carefree, innocent games along the shore, but only a few feet away Uncle and his friends build the small boat that they hope will carry them all to freedom from the soldiers and a life where they can find work and food to survive.

Temple depicts life in Haiti before democracy was restored so that young readers can understand. A group meets secretly to listen to a radio broadcast, because it's illegal for more than four people to gather together. Both Karyl's father and the local teacher are in hiding because of their political beliefs. No one dares to mention the exiled, former president, Aristide.

In this repressive environment, Karyl's older brother, Jean-Desir, takes an enormous risk. When an American journalist questions him, he tells the truth about how harsh life is and how the people need Aristide to return. Truth is indeed dangerous in Haiti and that night Jean-Desir is murdered.

Paulie is struggling toward adulthood. With Jean-Desir's death, she leaves behind the innocence of childhood. She decides that the "truest and hardest thing she could do for Jean-Desir" would be to go to Port-au-Prince and tell the truth about his death to the journalist. It is a risky journey and she barely escapes with her life.

Later, as the villagers sail to Florida in the small homemade boat, Paulie continues to wrestle with some of the big questions of life asking, "Is there any other way to defeat the people who would make you into slaves, or do you only just have to kill them?" Interestingly, none of the adults have an answer for her.

The book has a section that explains the historical context of the story, and although it is not absolutely necessary, I think readers will enjoy the book more if you read and talk about this with them first. There is also a good glossary for the many Creole words. Although Temple clearly had strong feelings about Haiti's quest for freedom, she managed to skillfully weave the politics into the story. There are deaths and danger, but these are not sensationalized. If anything, it seems to me that the boat trip to Florida could be better described with a more immediate sense of danger. There is also great sadness in this story, but it is coupled with a strong sense of the beauty of everyday life and the strength that comes from the closeness of family and friends.

In Temple's *Grab Hands and Run,* a book that is slightly easier reading, Felipe and his family escape from persecution in El Salvador and make the difficult journey through Guatemala to Mexico, across the border to the U. S. and on to Canada to begin a new life.

Felipe is a likeable character who is not only struggling to survive the journey but also to grow into a man. Like Paulie, he is wrenched from his childhood by the harsh circumstances of his life. Temple equates growing up with being able to make decisions. Felipe thinks that maybe growing up is "Not getting taller, but thinking for yourself. Questioning instead of just going along."

In a moving scene, Felipe must decide whether to return to El Salvador or to continue on to Canada with his mother and sister. "Growing up isn't something you necessarily want to do…. Growing up is something you decide to do. It takes courage." Although Felipe desperately wants to return to fight for his country's freedom, it takes more courage for him to go on to Canada and get an education so he can return as an adult better prepared to truly help his country.

Temple weaves together details of life in El Salvador with the suspense of the difficult journey. The danger of being caught crossing borders, the difficulty of having only a limited amount of money, the treachery of unscrupulous people, and finally the fear of being sent back to a country where the soldiers have murdered his father are all well described. Not even adults are always sure of what to do, but they somehow find the courage to choose. This is what Felipe learns at the heart of this compelling story.

Lauren read this book and was amazed to learn that in some countries boys as young as twelve could be taken into the army. She liked the book's suspense and the way the family never gave up. "I would recommend it for ages 8-88," she said in an enthusiastic burst of approval. The book was also well liked by a group of sixth and seventh graders who read and discussed it.

• Journey of the Sparrows

Journey of the Sparrows, written by Fran Leeper Buss with the assistance of Daisy Cubias is also about a family who escapes from El Salvador after the father and older sister's husband have been killed by the Guardias. In a memorable opening scene, 15-year-old Maria and three other young people make the journey over the Mexican border nailed into a fruit crate. This scene would make an excellent read-aloud during a study of refugees.

Details of everyday life in El Salvador are told through flashbacks as Maria recalls her life as a young girl. These memories contrast with the difficulties of life as an illegal alien in Chicago. At first it seems anything is possible in the land of freedom, but the harsh reality of being illegal soon becomes apparent. There are no legal recourses when Maria's boss attempts to molest her so she is forced to quit her job. Rather than have her illegal status discovered and risk being sent back to El Salvador, her sister must have her baby at home despite complications. They survive with the help of other illegal aliens and American church groups. Then

Maria returns to Mexico to rescue her baby sister and must again cross the border. This is a sad book, but its somber mood is somewhat relieved by Maria's memories, the closeness of the refugee community, her blossoming relationship with Tomas, and her strength and perseverance.

• Lupita Manana

A similar story is *Lupita Manana* by Patricia Beatty. Lupita and her older brother, Salvador, leave their small Mexican village and cross illegally into the U.S. to try to find work to help support their family. As in the previous two books, the dangers of crossing the border are dramatically described. Lupita and Salvador are beaten by robbers and shot at before they manage to cross the border. They find their way to their aunt's house in California and begin working in the fields picking vegetables. Like Maria in *Journey of the Sparrows,* they live in fear that they will be caught by immigration officers and sent back to Mexico.

As Salvador and Lupita grow apart, she feels increasingly alone in this alien land. She decides that she must "make a skin for herself against a world that could be so suddenly and unexpectedly cruel…a shell so hard that nothing could pierce it…"

Just as the reader begins to despair that Lupita's life will ever improve, she decides that she must learn to speak English. Her young cousin, Irela, becomes her teacher. Beatty ends with these words, "Let the other Ruiz cousins laugh at them both. That would mean nothing to her or Irela. Both of their tomorrows were sure to be better." Although this ending seems to oversimplify the solution to Lupita's problems, the book is well worth reading. Beatty has created a heroine who makes the difficulties of being uprooted from her home and family to try to make a better life, come alive for young readers.

Kendra, a sixth grader, wrote, "Their lives were so much different than ours. They don't get enough food, they have to work at age 13, they can't go to school and their lives are much harder. I think this book is especially realistic because it doesn't have a happy ending. I would rate it a 9.5 on a 1-10 scale."

Alison, another sixth grader, enjoyed *Lupita Manana* because "it moved quickly and was very interesting. You learn a lot about what it is like for Mexicans who want to come to the United States. I never realized that it was so hard for poor Mexicans to make money. Our school collected money for people in Honduras who could have been poorer than Lupita's family. I wish I had given more."

• The Storyteller's Beads

Several other books deal with the theme of a long and difficult journey to make a better life. *The Storyteller's Beads* by Jane Kurtz is the story of two Ethiopian girls who escape from famine, violence, and persecution to a new life in Israel. For the first half of the book, the chapters alternate between the stories of two characters – Rahel, a blind Ethiopian Jew, and Sahay, who belongs to the Kemant people. They come from different villages and do not know each other when the novel begins.

Sahay has been taught all her life to fear and look down on the Ethiopian Jews, but when she and her uncle flee impending violence, she finds herself traveling in the company of a group of Jews who are also escaping. They must cross the rugged terrain of northern Ethiopia, climb mountains, cling to narrow paths on the edges of cliffs, and avoid both government troops and bandits.

Near the Sudanese border, the group is stopped by Ethiopian soldiers, and the men are forced to return to join the army. The women and children go on alone to a Red Cross refugee camp. Rahel has depended on her brother to guide her and now, despite her prejudice toward Jews (called Beta-Israel), Sahay takes his place. During their long struggle the two girls grow closer and come to know each other as individuals rather than as representatives of rival ethnic groups.

Life in the refugee camp is extremely difficult. People are dying of disease and, worse, of hopelessness. Sahay had "always looked to the elders in her family to tell her what to do. Now she had no one. All around her were people sitting, waiting, with silent, staring eyes that held no hope. *Waiting, waiting – for what? To die?*" But Sahay and Rahel are both stubborn survivors. Rahel carries only her flute and the storyteller's beads her grandmother gave her before she left. "The stories will keep you strong," her grandmother had told her. The stories themselves are woven into the text as Rahel tells them to bring herself and Sahay courage. Together, Sahay and Rahel help each other to survive.

The story ends as the two girls and others are airlifted by a Jewish relief agency to Jerusalem. This is based on the true story of Operation Moses, the first in a series of massive airlifts by the government of Israel that transported more than 6700 people to Israel in just two months in 1984. In that year alone ten to twelve thousand Ethiopian Jews left their villages in Ethiopia to go to Sudan. Kurtz provides an interesting chapter at the end of the book on the history of Ethiopia that led to the modern ethnic conflicts. She also includes a useful glossary of Amharic words that are used in the novel.

In *The Storyteller's Beads* the plot is condensed into a short 150 pages. The action moves swiftly, and we get an adequate, if not deep portrait of the characters. It's a good book for younger middle grade readers, although in some parts the sadness is quite intense.

• The Return
• Kiss the Dust

The Return by Sonia Levitin tells a very similar story and is a longer, somewhat more difficult book. It's about Desta, a young Ethiopian Jew who survives a treacherous journey from her mountain home to the refugee camps of Sudan. Desta, her older brother Joas, and her younger sister, Almaz leave their village and plan to join friends in the next village for the journey to Sudan. But when they arrive, the others have been forced by their guide to leave without them. The three siblings hurry on, hoping to meet up with the others. They travel for many days, worrying about running out of food and water and constantly fearing meeting soldiers or bandits.

Finally, in a heart-wrenching scene, Joas is shot by bandits as he returns from a scouting expedition. The two sisters watch him appear over the hill and then fall from the shot. Later, Desta remembers the moment "over and over, him standing to see all around and the shot ringing so, then the echo. I would hear that sound in my dreams forever. Forever I would see that small round hole in his back, and the circle of blood around it. So small a thing stands between life and death, a tiny round hole." Now Desta must take charge, and she and Almaz struggle on alone.

They finally meet up with the others, and they travel together. Levitin describes the long journey well, giving a sense of what it must have been like to walk day after day in the blazing heat. "Some days it was all I could do to bring down one foot after the other, with no strength for thoughts, shallow or deep. Yet other days sent me into a trance so pure that I forgot my body completely, my mind fastening upon a thought, then another, probing and twisting the way my fingers used to pick at the knots in a ball of twine. Then, hunger and thirst were forgotten; I caught a glimpse of what it must be like for holy men who live in meditation."

At last they cross the border into Sudan but not before one of the group has been captured by soldiers. Levitin's portrait of life in a refugee camp is one your students will not quickly forget. When they read news stories of the latest group of refugees in any part of the world, their acquaintance with Desta will put a human face on the suffering. I know that I will never be able to read about refugees again in quite the same way.

Like Rahel and Sahay, Desta and Almaz are finally rescued by Operation Moses and taken to Israel. This is a gripping survival story as well as a coming of age story. Levitin is a skilled writer who has created a likeable heroine who meets each new challenge with growing strength.

Nicole, a sixth grader, gave this book a strong endorsement. She wrote: "I loved it! The combination of loneliness and death, yet love and joy for reaching the Promised Land made an excellent story. Your mind felt the danger and felt what the characters felt. What amazed me was that they were digging up clay and making their own pots, their own houses, their own everything when we were here, within a mile of a grocery store, with a TV or two in our house, and we're taking all this for granted! It's sickening! It brought up a lot of feelings, and it really made me wonder."

TEACHING IDEA

If you're planning to have groups of students read books about refugees it would be interesting to begin by reading aloud a chapter that is set in a refugee camp. *Kiss the Dust, The Return,* and *Goodbye Vietnam* all have interesting scenes set in camps that give a feel for the difficulty of life under such conditions.

Elizabeth Laird's *Kiss the Dust* is set in Iraq and is similar in some ways to *The Return*. The story opens when Tara and her friend witness a young Kurd shot down by the police for reading subversive material on the street. The incident changes Tara who is also Kurdish and makes her realize she is a member of a minority living in a hostile land. Her father is a leader in the Kurdish freedom movement, and the family barely escapes from the secret police. They leave their wealthy life in the city and go to their summer home in the mountains.

Tara has a difficult time adapting to life in the small mountain village. At first she is contemptuous of the simple life the villagers lead. When the old woman next door saves her life during a bombing raid she realizes, "When bombs start falling, it didn't matter how good you were at [math], or how rich your father was. The only important things were how brave you were, and how generous, and whether or not you could still have a good laugh."

Just as she is feeling comfortable in her new home, the family is forced to flee again. A dangerous journey over the mountains into Iran almost ends in tragedy when Tara falls off a bridge into a freezing river and is nearly swept away by rapids. Luckily, her brother rescues her.

In Iran they become refugees in two successive camps. They have lost their freedom, and both her parents have as much trouble adjusting as Tara herself. She realizes she must find her own strength. The story ends on a hopeful note when the family eventually reaches England and starts to rebuild their lives.

The story is interesting, the picture of life in a refugee camp is vivid, and the information on the Kurds is valuable for students. For me, it lacked the emotional punch of *The Return*. Perhaps this is because it is written in third person instead of first. Perhaps Laird is a bit too didactic for my taste and has made Tara an instrument for a lesson on the plight of the Kurds rather than a character with the depth of Desta. But it's still good reading, and the students who read it rated it highly.

TEACHING IDEA

Send students to the Internet and the library to find information on the Kurds. Some questions you might want to have them investigate include:

- What was life like for this group of people in their country of origin?
- What led to people having to flee their homeland? (historical background)
- Can you find any pictures from the time when the character fled her country?
- Are refugees still coming from this area? If not, what has changed?
- Where have the majority of refugees gone? What is life like for refugees in these countries?
- Have people's lives improved or gotten worse?
- What is happening today in their country of origin? Would it be safe to return?

You could use this strategy with any of the ethnic groups described in books in this chapter.

• The Clay Marble

In *The Clay Marble* by Minfong Ho, Dara and her family journey across western Cambodia to a refugee camp on the border with Thailand, trying to escape the war that has killed their father. This is a story of refugees, but it is even more the story of a friendship. At the huge Nong Chan camp, Dara and Jantu become close friends. They escape the difficulties of life by creating a miniature village of tiny clay figures. Dara says, "...the toy village became the center of our world… In our small make-believe world, at least, life was simple and easy to understand. There were no soldiers and no war, only people like ourselves quietly getting on with their lives."

Ho keeps the story moving. When fighting erupts on the border, the camp is shelled, and Dara and Jantu and their families become part of a mass exodus. They become separated from their families, then from each other, and finally Dara returns alone to the refugee camp, hoping her family will come back to find her. She discovers their toy village destroyed, the days of innocence gone forever. She eventually makes her way to another camp and finds her family.

When her older brother decides to join the fighting, Dara takes charge and begins preparations to return to their village. Tragedy strikes, and Jantu is killed. Dara discovers inner strength she didn't know she had and moves on with her life without Jantu.

Ho has written a quiet story of a friendship, of life and death, and hope. The writing is excellent and smooth; it pulls you easily into Dara's world and does not have sensationalized, gory scenes.

Alessandra, an eighth grader who enjoys realistic fiction, read this book during the NATO conflict in Kosovo in the spring of 1999 and found herself thinking frequently of the Albanian refugees as she read. She gave the book a high rating. "It gave a really good picture of what it's like to live in a war-stricken country, always having to run for safety. The author didn't pump the story with a lot of guts and glory. It was actually a pretty mellow book compared to others of its type. It didn't show you all the blood and action of war. It showed what life was like for the people who weren't fighting, for the innocent civilians who were dragged into the middle and who were made to suffer.

One really powerful part was when Jantu got shot. Can you imagine how horrible that would be? To have your friend killed? Not only that, but to have her killed by one of your own people, by someone who was on your side? This really showed me how awful war could be. You always hear about the poor soldiers who die in the heat of battle, but you rarely ever hear of the civilians who die for no reason. This book really got the message across that you don't have to be a soldier to suffer from war."

TEACHING IDEA

Invite people in your community who have been forced to flee their homelands to talk to the class about their experiences. You may be able to locate them through a refugee resettlement program, social service agencies, or local church groups. Have small groups of students interview each guest. I did this several years ago, and students were fascinated to hear their stories. Later, students can share what they've learned by writing profiles of their interviews.

• Goodbye Vietnam

Goodbye, Vietnam, by Gloria Whelan is another good book for younger middle school readers. After the Vietnamese War, Mai and her family escape from their small Vietnamese village to Hong Kong. Forty people are crowded into a small boat with not even enough space to stretch out full length. There is little food or water. Mai's father is a mechanic who tries desperately to keep the ancient motor running. They have no decent map, and no one is even sure they're heading in the right direction. Despite the difficult conditions, Mai and her family survive, and, in one of my favorite parts, celebrate Tet with the other passengers.

When they finally arrive in Hong Kong they are herded into a huge warehouse filled with other refugees and given a small area on a platform in which to live. They begin a long wait for someone to sponsor them in the U. S.

Although the more gruesome details occur offstage, there is still a strong sense of danger and desperation. They rescue a young boy from the sea whose entire family has been killed by pirates. The old man next to them on the boat dies. Many people at the warehouse are shipped back to Vietnam against their will. Younger readers will enjoy this simply written, but excellent story. A sixth grader, wrote to me after reading several books about refugees, "I think it was one of the best books I've read so far. I never wanted to put it down. It seemed so real to me."

TEACHING IDEA

Another question which students might like to explore is "How do refugees adjust to life in a new country?" There are a number of good books on this topic, and it could become an entire study of its own.

Inevitably, the characters in these books feel a conflict between the values of their own culture and those of their new country. The normal adolescent struggle to find an identity is complicated by the conflict of values. In each of the following books the message is clearly that the newcomer can combine the best of both worlds although none says exactly how this difficult task is to be accomplished. Some of the best include:

Skateway to Freedom by Ann Alma. Josie and her family escape from East Germany and try to start a new life in Canada. This simply written book clearly shows the difficulties of adjusting to life in a different culture from learning a new language to making friends.

Children of the River, by Linda Crew. Sundara is caught between her desire to meet the expectations of her Khmer culture and her growing attraction to an American boy. This book will interest more mature readers. Both boys and girls have liked this novel. One student wrote, "This book is probably one of my all time favorites!"

Shadow of the Dragon, by Sherry Garland. At home Danny Vo lives a traditional Vietnamese life. At school he wants the beautiful Tiffany to go out with him, but her brother is a member of a white supremacist gang who hates Asians. For more mature readers.

Thief of Hearts, by Lawrence Yep. Stacy is half American and half Chinese. In the course of a few days she learns much about her mother, her grandmother, her Chinese heritage, and most of all, about herself.

Join In: Multi-ethnic Short Stories edited by Donald R.Gallo. Great read-aloud stories about recent teen immigrants as well as second and third generation Americans. See review in Chapter 4.

• The Spirit Catches You and You Fall Down
• Monkey Bridge
• Arranged Marriages
• Interpreter of Maladies

There are a number of excellent adult books that you might enjoy reading to broaden your understanding of this topic. One of the best books I've ever read is *The Spirit Catches You and You Fall Down* by Anne Fadiman. Winner of the National Book Critics Circle Award, it is the true story of a cultural clash between a small county hospital in California and a Hmong refugee family from Laos over the treatment of the the young daughter's epilepsy.

Monkey Bridge by Lan Cao is a novel about a young Vietnamese immigrant building a new life in America after the war. Her story alternates with her mother's story of life in Vietnam and provides a contrast between the two cultures.

Two wonderful fictional accounts of Indian women trying to keep their traditional values and at the same time make a place for themselves in their new American lives are *Arranged Marriages* by Chitra Banerjee Divakaruni and *Interpreter of Maladies* by Jhumpa Lahiri. Both are collections of short stories.

Charlotte, a sixth grader, wrote to me in a reading letter: "I think that if you don't read, then you're missing out on something very important and exciting. Reading is like going to different worlds and meeting interesting people...Sometimes reading helps me understand other people's minds and their lives. I love reading because it stretches my mind to its limit."

Charlotte's incredible testimony made me think about the relationship between reading literature and social studies. I want my students to be "citizens of the world." I want them to be knowledgeable about current events and the historical forces that shape those events. Even more importantly, I want them to care about the lives of others. And I know that simply reading a textbook, or reading and watching the daily news is not enough to accomplish this goal. I know that to truly be a global citizen you must understand the lives of people in different cultures.

As Charlotte, at 12, so wisely knows, through good literature we can feel the connection between our lives and theirs; we can begin the process of understanding so that the young Mexican crossing the border into the U.S. or the Cambodian teenager in a refugee camp is no longer a stranger to us.

Reading is not like something extra. It's part of my life. I think I like it just because I get to meet people I never would and see how they feel.
                                                          — Zina Ward, Grade 6

Chapter 6: Bruised and outside
— Novels about the homeless —

They live in tents down by the tracks, a small community of outsiders. At noon some straggle up to the soup kitchen in the center of town and line up to get a decent meal. When winter winds whip across the hills, they retreat to the local shelter or huddle by the heat vents behind the stores on Main Street. They are down on their luck, bruised by life, outsiders in a land of affluence. You can find them in any part of America, urban, rural, and in-between. They are the homeless, and each has a story to tell.

I knew that homelessness continues to be a problem throughout the U.S. despite decades of effort, and I wondered how I could help my students to grow up to be part of the solution. How could I encourage fifty middle graders, the majority of whom are living well-fed and warm and safe in middle class suburbia, to think about those who are hungry and cold and living in constant fear of where the next meal and the night's shelter will come from?

I thought the answer might lie in reading novels. There are a surprising number of young adult novels that give an intimate portrait of the inner landscape of people who are trapped in hopelessness. For some characters it is born of poverty. Other characters are teenage runaways who find themselves outside the love and security of a family. All survive by finding a new community where belonging banishes despair. I hoped that when my students read these books they'd begin to develop compassion for the lives behind the statistics in the daily news.

• Slake's Limbo

One of the earliest young adult books about a homeless child is *Slake's Limbo* written by Felice Holman in 1974. In the first few pages, Holman reveals Slake's situation. In school the victim of bullies, at home the victim of a loveless household; Holman says, "There was no one for

Slake." With those cold words we can picture the desperate life of this boy who has been given nothing and who has no expectations, a boy outside any community of warmth and caring. One day when he can stand it no longer, he escapes into the New York subway system. The book is the record of his 121-day survival below ground.

By luck, Slake finds he can collect used newspapers on the subway and re-sell them. With the money he earns each day, he buys a sandwich from a coffee shop and explores the subway routes. He establishes a daily routine that gives him comfort. He scavenges discarded things to create a home in a hole in a subway tunnel where, for the first time in his life, he has a space to call his own, a haven from a world of violence and anger.

Slake is the main character, and there are only a small number of minor characters. One of my students commented that "By not having very many characters at all, it gets the reader feeling that Slake is not part of the world." There is indeed an intense sense of his isolation. Slake is basically alone, although there are people who help him, and he gains courage from their kindness. One of his regular customers, a cleaning lady, brings him a winter jacket. The waitress at the coffee shop gives him extra food. And ultimately, when he is too sick to save himself, a subway train driver rescues him from the tracks.

Despite the kindness of these adults, and despite Slake's own inner will and strength that enable him to survive, there is a terrible bleakness about this book. On one level it's a survival story as surely as Gary Paulsen's *Hatchet,* and while some of my students felt it didn't have enough action, others liked it for the thrill of seeing how Slake managed to survive. Liz, a seventh grader, wrote, "One of the reasons this story appealed to me is it wasn't yet another survival story in dense woods but exactly the opposite. The station was a bustling, busy place full of people." Would 21st century teens be able to live as Slake did? Some of my students thought the solitude would be too hard to bear.

On a deeper level *Slake's Limbo* is a modern fable asking the difficult question – what does it mean to live completely outside a community with no one to love or be loved by? How many children today are in situations like Slake's – if not physically isolated, then just as alone emotionally? What should we do to help? Holman gives no answers but does end the book on a small note of hope. When Slake leaves the hospital, Holman tells us he has been reborn, and instead of returning to the familiar underground world, he gets off the subway. He "did not know exactly where he was going, but the general direction was up." With these words Holman ends the book. Slake has gained enough confidence in himself to risk life in a new environment. We would like to believe that if he could survive below ground for 121 days, he will be just as capable of making a new life, perhaps a better life, for himself above ground in a world where he can see the sky.

> **TEACHING IDEA:**
> For many students, the world of the homeless is light years away from their own experiences. It's easy for those of us from different socio-economic backgrounds to form stereotypes of the homeless. To help combat this, I invited a social worker from the local homeless shelter and one of his clients to speak to the class. A well-dressed man with a college degree spoke about the bad choices he'd made that had led to his living on the streets. "It really could happen to anyone, couldn't it?" mused one student afterwards.

• No Turning Back

Beverley Naidoo's *No Turning Back* is set in Johannesburg, South Africa. Sipho, the young black hero, who lives in post-Apartheid South Africa, has a mother who is struggling with her own problems and can't take adequate care of him. Sipho runs away when life with his abusive stepfather becomes unbearable and finds a community of other runaways.

In Johannesburg, life on the streets is not easy. Hunger and cold are constant threats. He sleeps on a thin piece of cardboard, huddled together with others in the gang he's joined. At one point he even sleeps in a garbage can, a scene that one student felt "really showed the brutal side of being homeless." Sipho earns enough money to buy a little food by pushing shopping carts or parking cars. When the cold and hopelessness overcome him, the temptation is strong to take drugs. His friend Joseph is a glue sniffer and Sipho is attracted to it. Luckily, his friend Jabu rescues him by convincing him of the stupidity of getting hooked.

There are dangers everywhere. "I would be very scared if that was me," commented one student. A group of older homeless men who are drunk pose a serious threat, and an older, stronger boy in the same gang steals Sipho's money. But more dangerous still, is a group of out-of-uniform police officers and their friends who don't like the changes in South Africa. They capture the gang of boys and take them to a nearby lake. "Rubbish like you can get a nice wash here," they yell as they throw them into the ice cold water. Many, like Sipho, can't swim. Again, luck is on his side and Jabu, who is a strong swimmer, rescues them all.

Then Sipho's life changes abruptly. He is befriended by Mr. Danny, a White man, and his daughter who offer him a job and a place in their home. He gains security, a warm bed of his own, and more than enough to eat. But he misses the freedom of the street life and feels the awkwardness of his position in a White family. Although he is treated well, Mr. Danny's prejudice and the outright hatred of his son lurk just beneath the surface cordiality. When he is unjustly accused of stealing from Mr. Danny, he runs away. A student who was thinking of how he would feel if he were in Sipho's shoes, said, "If it was my choice I would choose to stay and have safety, food, and shelter rather than having freedom." This became an interesting point for discussion among the students who had read this book.

Once again, Sipho is lucky. He finds Jabu at a local shelter and is persuaded to stay there, too. As several students who read this book concluded, "He's just in the right place at the right time or he's in the wrong place at the wrong time, but none of it seems to be in his control." The book ends with Sipho going to school and hoping an education will help him make a better life for himself. He sees his mother and gains an understanding of the pressures she is trying to cope with. He hopes that someday they can be together again.

Although life on the streets seems a bit too cozy sometimes, there are enough details to outweigh these infrequent times. The book, which Naidoo says is based on real life stories of young Blacks living on the streets, is appropriate for younger readers at the same time that it's interesting to more mature readers. The story moves swiftly, and you quickly come to care about what happens to Sipho. One of my students wrote, "The author told this story in such a way that I could relate to Sipho's feelings. I understood how he was feeling and the choices he made."

There are a number of other books about homeless children set in other countries that I have discussed elsewhere in this book. There's Djo in *Taste of Salt*, trying to find himself in the chaos of modern Haiti (see Chapter 4). There are also the books that vividly describe children in refugee camps, victims of war and ethnic hatred (see Chapter 5). Desta is a young Ethiopian Jew in a Sudanese refugee camp in *The Return*. Dara, a Kurdish refugee, in *Kiss the Dust,* copes with the hardships of an Iranian camp. *The Clay Marble* deals with Cambodian refugees who are torn from their homes and must find a new home, a place where they belong, and a place where they are safe.

• The King of Dragons

In *The King of Dragons* by Carol Fenner, Ian and his father, a Vietnam War veteran, have been homeless for several years. His father has taught Ian how to survive. "Pull back; stay out of sight; don't leave a trace," is his father's code. When the book opens they're living in a huge abandoned city courthouse, which because of its designation as an historical landmark, has been kept in good repair and heated in the winter. The building has long hallways with warrens of offices and two huge courtrooms, bathrooms and even a shower. Fenner describes the building so well that the setting takes on a life of its own.

One night Ian's father doesn't return, and Ian is forced to live by himself. Unbeknownst to Ian his father has had an emotional breakdown and is in a hospital with no memory of who he is or his son. Fenner allows the reader to see the father's progress back to health through a series of brief scenes at the hospital.

The story of how Ian scrounges for food, finds a winter coat, tries to follow his father's code, and fights off his loneliness and fear makes for a compelling story. The details of his daily life are interesting, and there is enough suspense to satisfy younger middle school readers.

The story takes a twist when the building is turned into a museum and people begin to set up an exhibit of international kites. As Ian, in hiding, watches, he slowly comes to know the workers. He especially likes Jean, a bright high school drop-out in rebellion against her high powered mother. This adds another layer of complexity to what would otherwise be simply a survival tale.

At night when the building is empty, Ian reads about the kites and admires them, especially a beautiful Chinese one called the King of Dragons. Then Ian inadvertently reveals his presence. He convinces the museum people that he is being home schooled, and before he quite knows what has happened, he has a job guiding people through the kite exhibit and a budding friendship with Jean. Although this is all a little too coincidental for my taste, students who read the book liked it and thought it possible that Ian's life could take such a sudden turn for the better.

The book ends on an optimistic note when Ian's father returns, and although he is not quite well enough yet to take care of Ian, forcing Ian to live with his aunt for awhile, we feel confident that he and his father will soon have a settled life together. Ian is a sensitive and resourceful character whom students like.

TEACHING IDEA

Middle grade students can easily get discouraged when reading about the lives of the homeless. They need a sense that it's not completely hopeless and that there are things being done in the community. I sent student teams into the community to interview people at local and state agencies about the services they offer, the problems they encounter in their work, and the trends they've noticed in recent years.

The agencies we visited included a state program to provide food and financial aid to women with infants and children, the food shelf, Women Helping Battered Women, Habitat for Humanity, Legal Aid, a drug and alcohol treatment center, the Salvation Army, an agency that helps runaway teens, a state housing assistance office, a local shelter, and a program that works to provide free breakfast programs in schools.

Students shared what they had learned with the other members of the class.

• Monkey Island

Paula Fox's *Monkey Island* gives the most realistic picture of life on the street of any of the books I've mentioned so far and is written with Fox's usual skill. However, I hesitate to recommend it, because several of my students found it too slow to get into and abandoned it. If you can match it with the right students it's a gem of a book, but it's not for everyone. When Clay's mother is overcome by mental illness and abandons him, he finds himself living on the street. In the park he is "adopted" by Buddy and Calvin, two homeless men who become his family. His relationship with Buddy is especially touching. As an icy winter descends on New York City, Clay, who is only 11, learns how harsh life is on the street. There are dangers not only from the cold and lack of food, but from gangs who attack them with chains and baseball bats.

Clay is stricken with pneumonia and winds up in the hospital. This causes him to be reunited with his mother and with a new baby sister, and they again try to make a home. Buddy tells him, "You're one of the lucky ones." Paula Fox has an uncanny ability to create realistic characters who take on a life beyond the pages of her books. Although I read *Monkey Island* several years ago, Clay, Buddy, and Calvin are still vivid in my mind.

• Mary Wolf

Mary Wolf by Cynthia D. Grant is the story of a homeless family. Sixteen-year-old Mary and her family have been on the road in their RV for almost two years. It started as a vacation after her father lost his job and turned into an extended road trip on the way to a better life. But instead of getting better, life only gets worse. Her father gets menial jobs only to lose them a few weeks later because he's been caught stealing or has yelled at the boss. Her mother steals from stores and sells the goods at flea markets. Mother "masks her thoughts even from herself," Mary observes.

Mary tries to take care of her three younger sisters and her new baby brother as well as cope with her father's increasing anger and violence. For a short time the children go to school, but they are clearly outsiders, looked down on because they are poor. It is not an easy life.

Although this is Mary's story, it is also the story of the downward spiral of a man into despair. At one point her father tells them he has a job as maintenance man for a development of summer homes, and the job provides a free home. They move into a luxurious, completely furnished home. The family's hopes rise only to be shattered when they discover that he lied and they are living without permission in someone's summer home.

A group of girls who read this book were very angry with the father. Both their reading logs and their group discussions reflected their feelings. One girl wrote, "I think the father is becoming an alcoholic because he thinks that getting drunk will solve all of the family's problems, but it's not. Their problems are only getting worse. And it's really messing up the family." This girl, by the way, had told me numerous times in both words and actions that she didn't like to read. Until *Mary Wolf,* she had never finished an assigned book. When I praised her for finishing *Mary Wolf* and participating in the group discussion as well as completing her log, she told me that she had really liked this book. "Do you have any more books like this?" she asked.

Another student showed her annoyance with Mr. Wolf by referring to him by his first name, Andrew, in her log. "Andrew has such a big ego problem. My gosh, Andrew, don't talk to your wife that way. If I were your wife, I'd be terrified...I'm glad Mary brought the baby to the clinic without her father knowing. Good for her!"

Still another girl wrote, "I can't believe they all listen to Mr. Wolf's pitiful little apologies over and over again. Something has to happen. Don't they realize that?"

About halfway through the book they end up at River's End, a run down campground populated with other people without jobs living in campers or tents or driftwood shacks. Mary becomes friends with a boy her age, and their relationship adds a little lightness to a somewhat depressing story. In her log, Danielle wrote about her reaction to Mary's first boyfriend: "Wow! They kissed. I thought that might happen but not that soon."

Although everyone is happy to settle down for awhile, River's End becomes the end of the line for the family. Grant has created an unexpectedly explosive ending to this compelling story. While trying to defend her family, Mary kills her father. While this scene was no problem for my seventh and eighth graders, I'd hesitate to recommend the book to most sixth graders.

As the book ends, there is hope that Mary's strength will enable her to create a better life. However, one can't help but wonder if she will ever be able to put what happened at River's End behind her.

All the students who read this book seemed to be personally involved in the story. Their logs reflected their emotional involvement with Mary and her family. Becky wrote, "Mary's dad confuses me. One minute he is a monster, the next he is a sweet father. First, I want to jump into the book and pound his brains out, but then I suddenly don't feel like that." In an emotional response to the ending, she wrote, "The ending is so sad. I don't think I know what to write except that I'm happy to remember that I live in a nice house with great parents."

In tribute to Grant's realistic writing, one student observed, "The characters in this book keep getting more and more aggravating. Are they "good" or "bad"? This is one of the first books I've read where that hasn't been too spelled out. I kind of like that; it's more realistic in a way. On the other hand, it's annoying not to be thinking the main characters are automatically wonderful!"

• Make Lemonade

In Virginia Euwer Wolff's *Make Lemonade,* the characters are not homeless but rather deeply rooted in the poverty that often leads to homelessness. Jolly is a single mom who needs a babysitter for her two young children so she can work the evening shift. LaVaughn lives with her mother in a neighborhood that is poor and dangerous and needs a part-time job to support her big dream of going to college. LaVaughn tells the story in free verse. Several students who read this book reported that they quickly got used to Wolff's free verse style.

When she first arrives at Jolly's to babysit LaVaughn says,
"Here's how it was at Jolly's house:
The plates are pasted together with noodles.
And these rooms smell like last week's garbage.
And there isn't a place I can put my book to study for school
Except places where something else already is."

She is horrified by Jolly's situation because she knows she is only inches away from ending up in such a place herself. "If I get out of here to college, I'll get a good job…and I'll never see a place like this again."

LaVaughn's mother is a strong, hardworking woman with a powerful will to make something of her life and to raise a daughter who can overcome her background and succeed. She believes Jolly is not "taking hold" and worries that she's "got hold of" LaVaughn and is not a good example. Indeed, LaVaughn is captivated by both Jolly and her children. They laugh themselves silly, and they begin to share confidences. Jolly tells about her previous life living in boxes. LaVaughn tells about how her father died in a random shooting during a gang war. LaVaughn has found a family to laugh and have fun with, a family that contrasts sharply with her hardworking, serious mother. But LaVaughn loves her mother and never forgets the goals she taught her.

"And I know nobody on TV is going to do my homework
and I don't want to do it either;
all those maps and semicolons
and binomials; but they're my ticket out of here;
so I pick up my books and get my stuff…"

When Jolly loses her job, LaVaughn longs to be able to work some magic to help. But there is no magic in Wolff's world, only guts and hard work. Wolff pulls no punches at showing the difficulties of raising two children alone with few resources – no family or friends to offer support, no savings, and no high school diploma to help in the job search. She shows how easy it is to fall into despair and lose hope.

LaVaughn continues to babysit for Jolly without pay and eventually takes Jolly to school with her. Jolly begins a GED program and slowly begins to pull her life together.

Then there comes a day when Jolly doesn't call anymore. LaVaughn says, "It's all completely different now, I been broken off, like part of her bad past. I was the one that knew the saddest parts of Jolly, I guess." The book ends as it began, a mixture of sadness and hope. Wolff makes her message clear. When life gives you a lemon, you have to make lemonade. LaVaughn even plants a lemon pit for Jolly's young son that by the end of the book has grown into a lemon plant.

A seventh grade girl who read this book told me that she found the first fifty pages "pretty slow, but later on I couldn't put the book down. There were a lot of things going on and it was a really good book!"

I heard Wolff speak at a conference several years ago, and she said she likes to write about outsiders, the "lonely outsiders with the grit to succeed." She has surely done a masterful job in creating Jolly and LaVaughn.

TEACHING IDEA

One day I invited three teen mothers, none much older than my students, to talk about their own lives and the choices they'd made. They spoke frankly of addiction to drugs and alcohol, of problems getting along with their parents. They testified to the difficulty of raising a baby, of stretching welfare payments to the end of the month, and of trying to finish high school. An eighth grader thought the speakers were an especially valuable part of our study. He said they convinced him far more than statistics that homelessness was a major problem.

• True Believer

For those who liked *Make Lemonade,* Virginia Euwer Wolff has written the second novel in a planned trilogy. *True Believer* continues with the next year of LaVaughn's life. On the first page, still writing in verse, Wolff describes simply, but eloquently, what adolescent life is like:

When a little kid draws a picture
it is all a big face
and some arms stuck on.
That's their life.

Well, then:
You get older
and you are a whole mess
of things,
new thoughts, sorry feelings,
big plans, enormous doubts,
going along hoping and getting
disappointed,
over and over again,
no wonder I don't recognize
my little crayon picture.
It appears to be me
and it is
and it is not.

Drawing by Kyle Norris

As LaVaughn makes her way through high school, her life made even more difficult by the poverty she struggles to overcome, she manages to hold fast to her dream of going to college.

The book seems to be written on two levels. One is the story of a 15-year-old girl's life, a story we can all identify with – adults through memories of our own difficult passage, and young adults who are struggling with the mysterious ups and downs of adolescence every day. LaVaughn tries to cope with a rift in her friendship with the two girls who have been her friends since childhood. They've joined a new church and urge LaVaughn to join, too. What does she believe? Is religion important in her life? LaVaughn struggles to find answers that make sense to her.

Meanwhile, she longs to find a boyfriend who will like "the real LaVaughn in me." Jody is a boy who lives in her apartment building and who makes her heart "too loud for comfort and my brain not so level either." When he talks to her, her "whole body goes twang." Yes, it is a crush to remind us all of our own first crush!

Like so many of our own students, LaVaughn worries about a lot more than just Jody and whether he likes her. She worries about the environment and about her mother's new boyfriend. She worries about going to the dance and whether a kiss is a real kiss or not. She worries about her lab partner and about the children who are dying in the cancer ward where she works after school. She comes to realize "How life is so thin and fragile, how you never know. One instant you're here and then you're gone."

On a second level, Wolff writes about what it takes to break out of poverty and into a better life. LaVaughn's mother warns her, "You cannot let yourself get confused…People are confusable…You keep your eyes on college." There is no missing Wolff's point that in order to succeed you need a good education. The going is tough, and Wolff minces no words about exactly how tough it is. LaVaughn is moved into a more challenging science class, and she signs up for an after-school grammar class to improve her English. She meets Artrille, a boy like herself, who plans to be a doctor. LaVaughn says, "Artrille is no richer than us. He lives in a slum like us. He would be valuable in a gang, he memorizes things well, He has quick eyes, they could scare you in a dark alley. And he's strong. He can lift Ronell with one hand. Artrille a doctor."

Another student asks him how he plans to become a doctor because it seems like such an impossible dream. Artrille's answer inspires LaVaughn: "I have never not worked since fourth grade. I always have a job, sometimes two. I can do it."

LaVaughn thinks: "Here's this plain American boy in a poor school in a poor place in an ugly time of people dying from guns and drugs and cruelty."

And even with hard work there are pitfalls and temptations along the way. For readers who live in LaVaughn's world, this is a book to show them the way and to inspire them the way Artrille inspired LaVaughn. For readers like my students, living their comfortable middle class lives, it's a book to help them understand the lives of others and to inspire them to take their own lives less for granted.

As LaVaughn turns 16, she gains a new insight into all the things that have been troubling her. She feels her own strength, and she tells herself she can "make it through another day" because she believes in something.

"I believe in possibility. In the possibility of possibility. Of the world making sense someday. That lump in my throat that keeps coming back to remind me of my messes, it only stays for a little while. I'm a true believer. And that's a fact."

There is no perfect world with an end to problems. There is only finding the strength to go steadily on toward your dreams. This seems to be Wolff's message, and it is clearly a message for us all no matter what our position in life may be.

• The Planet of Junior Brown

In *The Planet of Junior Brown,* Virginia Hamilton's Buddy finds a solution, his own version of the popular saying, "Think globally, act locally." So far, all the books I've discussed have been realistic, but *The Planet of Junior Brown* strikes me as different. Realistic in many ways, it is also somehow larger than life, almost like a legend.

In a secret room in the school basement, a homemade solar system glows softly in the darkness. Junior and Buddy hang out there with Mr. Pool, the janitor, and haven't gone to classes for months. Junior, who weighs over 300 pounds, is daily slipping closer to insanity. A gifted pianist, he seems increasingly unable to distinguish reality from fantasy.

Buddy is as tough and independent as Junior is vulnerable and dependent. He's part of a network of children who live on the street in groups called "planets." Older, more streetwise kids like Buddy get food, clothing, and shelter for the younger, newer kids. The older kids all go by the name "Tomorrow Billy." Legend has it that a group of homeless children once lived with a boy named Billy and each night when he left them in a safe, sheltered spot, they would ask, "Tomorrow Billy? Will you be back tomorrow?" He always answered yes and returned in the morning until finally, one night the children didn't ask. Billy realized they had learned to survive on their own and he never came back, moving on to help a new group of children. Buddy takes his role as a "Tomorrow Billy" seriously and believes his job is to help the children in his care learn to live for and by themselves.

But Buddy is soon to revise his ideas about his purpose in life. As Junior completely loses touch with reality, Buddy and Mr. Pool decide to save him. They take him to Buddy's "planet," a basement home in a deserted building, and lower him by a sling down to where Buddy's boys live. In a sudden flash of insight, Buddy sees clearly that they must learn to live, not for themselves, but for each other. They must help not only Junior, but each other, too. "We are together," Buddy tells them. "Because we have to learn to live for each other." He realizes that life is much more than "mere survival." They have become a family in the truest sense of the word, creating a place that is safe from the dangers of the world, helping each other to grow strong. Buddy's insight shines brightly into the darkness, a message for our times.

Weird? Yes. Wonderful? Definitely. This is not a book I'd give to most students to read independently. It's a story that needs mulling over, discussing, and then more discussing. In fact, one year I tried to interest several of my more mature readers in it and found only one who would read it. I was still convinced that Hamilton had written a masterful story that is well worth the effort of involving middle school readers, and the next year, I introduced it as a "very challenging book." A number of my best students eagerly signed up for it.

The discussion that followed was lively and thoughtful. Some students said they disliked the book and then, reluctantly, admitted that they hadn't really understood it. All agreed that it was weird. But the more we discussed the confusing parts, analyzed the meaning behind some of the scenes, and debated what the symbolism meant, the more they began to change their original perception of the book.

They all enjoyed the challenge of "analyzing" and agreed that Hamilton had done a great job on the "depth of the characters." They disagreed about the symbolism of the planets and the "red man" that Junior painted, but it is such disagreement that leads to deeper thinking and stronger effort on everyone's part to defend his/her perceptions. Everyone leaves with a deeper understanding of the book (including ME!) and this is what I love about book group discussions!

Interestingly, the next time I used the book with a group of students, they liked it right from the beginning. They admitted they didn't understand everything, but they, too, loved the process of figuring things out together. I learned a valuable lesson. Just as individuals differ in their taste in books, groups, made up of individuals, can also have different feelings about a given book.

• The Midwife's Apprentice

Although we sometimes think of homelessness as a late 20th century invention, there have been homeless children throughout history. There are four excellent historical fiction novels for middle grade readers that give a perspective of how different societies have treated their homeless – from Medieval Europe, to late 19th century Britain, to America in the 1850s, and during the Depression. Reading all four and making comparisons would be an excellent independent project for an ambitious student.

Karen Cushman's Newbery winner, *The Midwife's Apprentice,* is a brilliant portrait of a homeless girl in medieval times. When the book opens she is sleeping in a dung pile for warmth. She "knew no home and no mother and no name but Brat and never had." In a small village she is taken in by the midwife who is in need of cheap labor and slowly she begins to learn more than mere survival skills. She learns about singing, and making songs, and how to love a cat and a small boy in need of help. She learns many of the midwife's skills, and acquires a name for herself, Alyce.

As she spins the tale of Alyce's life, Cushman also vividly describes the medieval world of village and manor. Consider this paragraph describing Alyce's visit to the Saint Swithin's Day Fair:

> She passed through the forest of bright booths with flags and pennants flying, offering for sale every manner of wondrous thing – copper kettles, rubies and pearls, ivory tusks from mysterious animals, cinnamon and ginger from faraway lands, tin from Cornwall, and bright-green woollen cloth from Lincoln. She laughed at the puppets, wondered at the soothsayers, applauded the singers, and cheered for the racing horses. Her nostrils quivered at the smells of roasting meats and fresh hot bread and pies stuffed with pork and raisins, but her guts still trembled with excitement, and she was content just to smell.

But just as Alyce is settling in to her life as midwife's apprentice, she fails at her first attempt to deliver a baby alone, and unable to cope with her own failure, she runs away.

She gets a job at an inn where she learns about reading and writing and that it's okay to want something from life. When a visitor to the inn asks what she wants, she doesn't know. The idea of wanting something from life has never occurred to her. But after giving it some thought, she decides that what she wants is "A full belly, a contented heart, and a place in the world." Cushman seems to be asking, "Have the deepest desires of humankind really changed so much since medieval times?"

When Alyce successfully delivers a baby she decides she wants to be a midwife. She returns to the midwife to become her apprentice again, declaring "If you do not let me in, I will try again and again. I can do what you tell me and take what you give me, and I know how to try, and risk, and fail, and try again, and not give up. I will not go away." The midwife opens the door, and Alyce begins her new life. She has found her place in the world in a small village helping babies be born. The brat in the dung heap has come a long way.

Cushman has written a small book with a large, heartfelt message. She makes that message clear for young readers but writes in such a way as to charm older readers as well. A group of students, many with reading difficulties, who read this book enjoyed the story and found Alyce to be a very likeable heroine. Dan said he really liked "how strong and brave Alyce was." Lauren said that "Alyce got picked on by everyone, but she found her own friends. She was very independent. I could really identify with her!"

• Street Child

In 1837, Charles Dickens created Oliver Twist, perhaps one of literature's most famous children, to expose British society's savage neglect of abandoned and orphaned children. More accessible to middle grade readers than Dicken's classic, but just as revealing, is *Street Child* by British writer, Berlie Doherty.

Like many modern homeless families, Jim Jarvis's family encounters a series of events that set them on the path to eviction. First, his father dies, and then his mother becomes ill. Before he knows it he is separated from his sisters and put in London's dreaded workhouse, a place considered worse than prison by many. It is part asylum, where the mentally ill are caged, and part orphanage, where mischievous boys are whipped. Jim feels the loss of his family and his freedom and is determined to escape. "He would run and run through the streets of London until he was a long, long way from the workhouse. He would find a place that was safe. And he would call it home."

Unfortunately, finding a safe home is not an easy task, and Jim's journey is a grim one. As Jim moves desperately from one horrible situation to another Doherty reveals slices of Victorian life. After first escaping from the workhouse, Jim spends some time with Rosie, a friend of his mother's who lives on the banks of the Thames and sells fish. Rosie feeds him and cares about him. But this relatively secure life is shattered when Rosie's grandfather sells him to Grimy Nick who works on the river selling coal. He is a virtual slave to Nick and spends his days filling the hold of Nick's boat with coal from the ships outside the port and bringing it to a warehouse. "Backward and forward, filling and emptying, shoveling and piling, day after day after day."

But far worse than the hard labor is the lack of caring and hope in his life. "And never a word spoken between him and Nick. He would sleep on his hard bunk every night of his life. He would eat when Nick thought fit to feed him. He was Nick's slave, and he was treated worse than an animal." Indeed, when Nick catches him trying to escape, he ties a rope around Jim's neck each night the same way he ties his dog.

But Jim is strong, and he's smart, and before long he figures out how to escape without getting caught. For a short time he finds a home with an outgoing circus family. But this safety is also short-lived, and when he discovers the mother is about the sell him back to Grimy Nick, he runs away again.

He ends up on the streets of London, his faith in people almost destroyed. "He felt wretched, deep inside himself, black with wretchedness." He is reunited with his old friend, Shrimps, but Shrimps, a young child like himself, is dying. His search for a doctor for Shrimps leads him to Dr. Barnardo who runs a school for poor children. Although it is too late to save Shrimps, Jim's journey ends happily when Dr. Barnardo not only gives him a home but also starts a home for other street boys.

In the Author's Note at the end of the book, Doherty tells us that Dr. Barnardo was a real person who started the Ragged Schools in the 1860s and later opened a number of homes for destitute children. We learn that Jim, too, was a real person whom Dr. Barnardo credits with making him aware of the desperate situation faced by homeless children in London. The fact that the story is based on real people adds to its appeal.

• Jip: His Story

Katherine Paterson's *Jip: His Story* is set in rural Vermont in the 1850s. Jip is one of young adult literature's most lovable characters, and a story that many of my students have enjoyed. Although this is far more than a "homeless story," it can be used as one especially if you're trying to give students an historical perspective. When the story opens, Jip is living at a small town's poor farm, 19th century New England's way of dealing with people who couldn't care for themselves. Jip is a hard worker who is especially skilled with animals and people. He is gentle with both the cows and with his friend, Sheldon, of whom he says, "You ain't got extra sense, but you're lots stronger than most anyone." When Put, the "lunatic," arrives at the town farm, Jip is the only one who takes the time to get to know the educated man who is periodically subject to violent fits. He and Jip become close friends, and Jip cares for him during the times he's overcome with violence and must be caged.

The farm manager and his wife as well as the Overseer of the Poor, Mr. Flint, treat the residents as worthless castoffs, as objects, not people. In contrast, Jip's love and sensitivity can make modern readers think twice about their own prejudices. He says to his friend Lucy, "I wonder at people's ignorance. They said Sheldon was an idjit boy and Put a lunatic. We know better than that and we're only children."

Like the other residents of the town poor farm, Jip's self-esteem is weak, and he's convinced that he's not very smart. When Jip begins attending school, the new teacher helps him see that he is capable of learning. (If you've read Paterson's *Lyddie,* you'll recognize the spunky heroine back from college and teaching in a one-room schoolhouse!)

Just as Jip's life is taking a turn for the better, a menacing stranger appears in town looking for him. He claims to represent a man who believes Jip might be his long lost son. A series of shocking revelations follow and before long, Jip is on the run. The story builds to a strong and unexpected climax.

Eric, a discriminating seventh grade reader, loved this book for its "rich detail and description of historic Vermont." I agree with him that it's a wonderful book. Paterson has done an outstanding job of creating flesh and blood characters in a sad but realistic story that shows what life can be like when we take care of each other.

Like Hamilton's *The Planet of Junior Brown,* this is a story of the indomitablity of the human spirit. Both books speak passionately about the importance of helping each other, of the tremendous difference that reaching out to an outsider can make in that person's life.

• Nowhere To Call Home

You can learn a lot about what it was like to be a hobo during the American Depression in Cynthia DeFelice's novel, *Nowhere to Call Home.* The book begins with a gunshot that awakens young Frances Barrow, and in an instant her life of ease and wealth, her "safe, solid, and predictable" life is shattered. Her father has lost his fortune and committed suicide and Frances is destined to go to Chicago to live with her aunt.

In a moment of impulse, she decides to ride the rails. The family gardener had described the life of a hobo romantically as "...going wherever you please, sleeping out under the stars, free as the wind blowing past your face." Disguising herself as a boy, 12-year-old Frances hops into a dark boxcar and with incredulous luck meets Stewpot, a 15-year-old who's been tramping for three years. He teaches her the ropes – how to jump aboard a moving train, how to sneak past the bulls, the railroad cops who police the rail yards, and how to ask store owners for left over food. Overnight, Frances Elizabeth Barrow becomes Frankie Blue.

At first, life is exciting. They meet up with other hoboes at a "jungle," a small grouping of shelters, where they eat mulligan stew around a campfire and exchange stories. But life on the "rods," Frankie quickly learns, isn't as romantic as she'd thought it would be. Frankie and Stewpot are rounded up along with other hoboes and spend the night in jail. A night at a mission isn't much better, and Frankie is angered by the constant taunts they are subjected to by most of the people they meet. Before long, she is "tired and hungry and scared and homesick."

Just as she is thinking of giving up and going to her aunt's in Chicago, Stewpot's cold becomes worse and she knows that he needs her. She chooses to stay with him, and they head for Montana to see the Rockies. There's a great scene in which they watch, awestruck, from the open door of the boxcar as they pass the snow covered mountains. But during the long trip, Stewpot has become gravely ill.

They end up at Hooverville, a town for hoboes, in Seattle. Frankie's first look at Hooverville is shocking. "Crammed together were hundreds of dwellings made from every kind of unwanted scrap imaginable. People were living in rusted-out car and truck bodies, piano boxes, shacks fashioned from orange crates, ragged sheets of tin and canvas held together by broomsticks, saplings, junk metal and lumber, string and rope, and strips of cloth. Smoke from their wood fires hung in the damp, gray air."

Hooverville is the end of the line for Stewpot and his death fills Frankie with anger.

> "It's wrong, she gasped. All of – this." Her arms flew out, taking in the grave, the whole of Hooverville, the city of Seattle, and beyond. "He didn't have to die – he *shouldn't have died*!" Jack, a hobo they met in Hooverville, tells her that nothing can be done. "You say what's happening is wrong. Well, get used to it. The swells run the world. They're the ones who could make it better." He laughed abruptly. "If they wanted to."

But Frankie refuses to get used to a "world where poor people died in places like Hooverville. It seemed to her that Jack had given up, just as …her father had. They had let hopelessness move right into their hearts and take over. But Stewpot hadn't let that happen, and she wasn't about to, either." Frankie changes back into Frances and goes to live with her aunt, resolved to do something to help. This is a message that middle grade students with their idealism and desire to change the world can easily relate to.

One of the most interesting things about *Nowhere to Call Home* is DeFelice's use of hobo language. Words like frill, punk, Johnny Hollow Legs, and poundin' yer ear like a baby add authenticity to this detailed look at homelessness during the Great Depression.

All of these fast-paced and skillfully crafted novels, in addition to being good reads, are the stories of outsiders. The emotional content of these stories can speak to many middle school students who are trying to find their places in the tangled web of middle school relationships, and cliques, and sudden changes in friendships.

On another level, these novels raise the question of society's callous neglect of an entire segment of its population. They give students an intimate look at the world of the homeless, a territory as unfamiliar as a foreign country for most students. The stark images of poverty and the bleak reality of being alone and outside the safety of a community contrast sharply with the security of many readers' lives. Unless our students explore this territory, they can not begin to understand and grow into adults who can help make things better. As Hamilton's Buddy says so simply but eloquently, "…we have to learn to live for each other."

TEACHING IDEA

Students need to see that *they* can help. On four successive Fridays, groups of students spent an hour and a half at the Refugee and Resettlement Project, the Salvation Army, Ronald MacDonald House, the local food shelf, and Recycle North, a business that trains the homeless to repair appliances and then resell them to the community at reduced prices. Another group of students stayed at school and worked on "Project Angel Food," a national organization that collects unused food from restaurants. They organized a school-wide project to collect unopened milk cartons and uneaten fruit from the cafeteria to donate to Project Angel Food.

Students performed a variety of tasks including sorting clothes, hauling mattresses from one storage area to another, baking lasagna, cleaning rooms, shoveling snow, entering data on the computer, washing dishes, and stocking shelves.

Students enjoyed the work and looked forward to going back each Friday. An eighth grade boy who began his work at the Salvation Army with some skepticism wrote after his second visit: "One thing that surprised me was all the clothes they had. They had tons and tons of clothes. I learned how much hard work it is to sort them all and put them on the racks. I feel that I helped out a lot and really made a difference. I actually look forward to my next two visits."

A number of students asked me if we could continue doing it all year. Like all middle school students they liked the idea of getting out of classes, but I don't think that was their main motivation. They liked being a useful part of their community; they liked the feeling that came from knowing they were making a difference.

Conclusion

Looking for more books...

S o many books. So little time. You often hear people say this, and if you love reading, you understand its truth. I hope this book has inspired you to find books your students will love and will lead them to lively, thoughtful discussions.

Conversations I've had with students have helped me to realize how painful the changes and mysteries encountered in young adolescence can be. As they lay awake at night pondering the mysteries of their lives and of the world around them, they need books with well-developed characters who can serve as role models. They need authors who are not afraid to deal with sensitive issues. They need books that show them that they are not alone in their journey to become an adult. And most of all they need to be able to discuss these books – the characters, the issues, and the journey itself with other students and with adults.

"Lynn's been my best friend for five years and now she's dumped me," Becky sobs. "Now I have no friends left. Why does everyone hate me?" I try to offer some soothing words, and she drys her eyes and returns to class. The next day, she greets me with a big smile. She and Lynn have worked everything out and are friends again. The world of young adolescents changes daily. Up and down. Down and up. Tears and smiles. How can they learn to cope with this roller coaster ride, this explosion of emotions, in a healthy way?

"I don't want to be like my father."
"I want to be popular."
"I want to be perfect."
"I don't want to be known as a "nerd.""
"I don't know if I'm a compassionate person
or if I'm just mean at heart."

I've heard all these statements from different students this year. They wonder, Who am I? Where do I fit in? What really matters to me? What kind of person will I become when I'm grown up? How can students be thoughtful in their search for answers and find the courage needed to act on the answers?

––––––––––––

Sam is thrilled to be "going out" with Dawn. His best friend, Jim, is not thrilled by the new relationship in Sam's life. He doesn't like Dawn, plus he's hurt that Sam is sharing Jim's secrets with Dawn. Sam, on the other hand, is hurt by Jim's unkind words about Dawn and his daily pleadings for Sam to break up with her. Their friendship is on the verge of collapse, and both are unhappy. What does it take to maintain a friendship? What does it mean to be a true friend?

––––––––––––

A boy on our team is struggling with emotional problems. He sometimes says or does things that disturb other students. Students wonder what is wrong with him. There are many kinds of serious emotional problems that affect some of our students. Anorexia, depression, alcoholism, and obsessive-compulsive disorder are only a few of the illnesses that students struggle with. How can other students learn to understand and have compassion for them?

––––––––––––

As part of our African study, Maggie has been researching how the war in Sierra Leone has affected the hopes and dreams of children. The atrocities she's read about, child soldiers, refugees, rape, and death have shocked her and opened her eyes to the lives of children who have the same hopes and dreams she does, yet have been born in a war-torn country. She says, "We'll all go home tonight to our warm beds and our loving families. Why do we have so much and the children in Sierra Leone have so little?" How can students who have so much be inspired to think about and take action against both local and global injustice?

––––––––––––

Books are powerful tools. If we are familiar with many of the wonderful, well-written books that exist for middle grade readers, we can help to open doors onto new worlds and ideas. We can help them to better understand themselves and others. If we really listen to what they say, we can help to make a difference in their lives.

Drawing by Kyle Norris

When I'm reading, I get to know myself better."
— Maggie Satink, Grade 7

Appendix A

Parents and Students Read Together

It was a cold winter evening when 28 parents and their children gathered in my classroom to share their ideas about books. They broke up into four small groups to discuss books the students had chosen for themselves and their parents to read and spread out into adjoining rooms. Talk flowed easily. Laughter erupted in one group as they recalled a humorous scene. Another group quickly got into a lively debate about how the main character had changed. Later, disagreements emerged about the ending of one of the books. Some loved it. Others hated it. As the evening wound down, there was a feeling among both parents and students that the discussions had not only been fun, but the talk had drawn them closer together. "This was a good process to spend time together on something positive, something school-oriented and literary and not just TV," commented one parent. Students were equally enthusiastic. One said, "We had a wonderful conversation and I loved talking about the book and getting different perspectives. I like this a whole bunch!"

Organizing such an evening is easier than it may seem at first glance, and the benefits are well worth the effort. Here are some tips based on my experiences with a number of different family evenings.

First, you have to decide how many different choices of books you want to offer. When I first did this about ten years ago I had everyone read the same book. There are several problems with this approach. If a lot of people sign up, you'll need to buy a lot of copies of the same book. Also, the fewer choices you have, the fewer participants you're likely to attract and your goal is to engage as many families as possible.

How much control do you want to have over the books that are read? Do you want to choose the books yourself, or do you want to let students choose them? This is mainly a matter of your own comfort level and the availability of multiple copies of books. The most freewheeling approach is to let students organize themselves into groups with friends and select the book they want to based on the books you have available. Some groups may even be willing to buy their own copies if they don't like any of the books you have. The disadvantage of this approach is two-fold. Some students may want to participate, but none of their friends may be interested, so they have trouble finding a group to join. The other problem is that students may find it difficult to select a book that will lead to a rich discussion. On the positive side, this approach may lead to greater participation. I also think you can guide students in a way that will overcome these problems.

The method I like best allows for student choice, but gives me a little more control. I suggest four or five books and then let students add their suggestions to the list. Then I have students who are interested sign up for them. After sign-ups, I have to eliminate some books due to lack of interest, but that's okay. Students have the option of signing up to be with their friends but students whose friends are not participating are not placed in an awkward position.

Another thing to consider is collaborating with a teacher from another team. You'll have more participants, will be able to offer more variety of books and will have moral support for this new endeavor as well. If you want to really think big, consider doing what my colleagues in the grades 3-5 building in my district did. They organized a parent and student read evening for the entire school and wrote a grant to buy the books.

Now, which books to suggest or select? I have several criteria I use.

Quality: Seek books with well-developed characters and inspired, excellent writing.

Plot: Look for intriguing story lines that will interest both adults and students.

Conflict: Look for books with "meat" to generate discussion and perhaps some disagreement.

I like to also consider the overall selection and make sure there are books for a variety of interests and a variety of reading levels.

Here are some organizational tips:
- If you have to buy books, have people sign up first, then order the books. Wait until the books arrive to set the date for the discussion.
- Allow two to three weeks for people to read the book.
- Start the discussion at 7 p.m. and allow an hour or an hour and a half for the discussion.
- Consider asking students to volunteer to prepare cookies and punch to add some festivity to the evening.
- Organize the sign-ups so you have groups of 6-10 people. Less than six and the discussion won't be as rich. More than ten and people won't get enough chance to talk.
- Arrange for separate rooms for each group so they don't distract each other.

- Encourage students to sign up. I have often convinced some kids to come who were not originally interested.
- Your biggest task will be to create a discussion guide. When I first started this process I offered only a few books so I could create a custom guide for each book. I later discovered that you don't need specific questions in order to have a good discussion. I now use a list of general questions (see Appendix B) and suggest that people use it only as a guide. If your students are used to discussing books with others, they'll have no problem coming up with their own questions.
- You could ask a student in each group to serve as host/ess to welcome people and start off the discussion. In my experience, this is not really necessary. There's always someone in each group, sometimes a student, sometimes an adult, who gets things going. And there are always people who keep the conversation flowing.
- Send a written invitation to parents. They may encourage their child to participate.

On the evening of the discussion, your role is to be the host/ess. After everyone has arrived, give a brief welcome, announce room assignments, and hand out discussion guides. After people have dispersed, do a quick check of all the groups to be sure each discussion has begun. Help get the ball rolling if needed. After this, all you need to do is circulate. Sit for a few minutes with each group and see how the discussion is going. If you've planned well, they won't need you. Jump into the discussions if you want and create a little controversy if things seem too bland. Get an argument going and then move on!

Each time I've organized such an event, parents have always been appreciative of the opportunity to spend quality time with their child. "My son's perception were different than mine, so we both learned from the experience," said one mother. Students have also appreciated the chance to talk with and be listened to by adults. One student commented at the end of an evening discussion, "People really got involved. I liked how the adults related to us."

And, whenever people get together to talk about books, everyone almost always leaves with a feeling of having been enriched by the experience. One adult participant summed it up well when she said, "Our discussion was lively and I found others enjoyed different scenes in the book. The discussion gave me a new appreciation for those parts and a deeper enjoyment of the book."

Discussion Questions

1. How did each of you rate the book on a scale of 1-10 with #1 being the worst book you ever read and #10 being the best? Talk about why you rated it the way you did. Remember that you may have different opinions about the book, and that's okay. Respect each other's ideas even if you don't agree with them.
2. Were there any parts of the book that were confusing or that you didn't understand?
3. What is your favorite part or parts of the book?
4. Discuss the pace at which the story moved along. Did it move quickly and keep your interest? Did it drag and become too slow for your taste in some parts?
5. Could you picture the setting of the story?
6. Was there enough description throughout the book for you to picture the scenes, the action, and the characters? Or was there too much description for your taste? Find a sentence or paragraph that you think gives an especially good description of something or someone.
7. Who is the main character? Try to come to an agreement about this.
8. Did you like the main character? Could you identify with his or her situation?
9. What obstacles does your character face as he or she tries to overcome his/her problems?
10. Are these obstacles the result of bad luck? Other people's actions/choices? The character's own actions/choices?
11. Does your character resolve his/her problems? If not, why not? If yes, how? Does he or she resolve them through luck, through the intervention of someone else? Through his or her own actions? EXPLAIN!
12. Describe the kind of person your character is. Tell at least three good words to describe him or her.
13. How does your character change from the beginning to the end of the book? Discuss this change and what causes it.
14. How did you like the ending of the book? Do you think the author tied it up in a satisfying way? If not, what would have been a better way to end it?

15. What are the themes of the book?
16. Would you consider reading another book by this author? What else has the author written?

Appendix C

List of Publishers

Chapter 1: Against the Tide
Novels about standing up and speaking out

TITLE	AUTHOR	PUBLISHER
The Cuckoo's Child	Suzanne Freeman	Listening Library
Who Do You Think You Are? Stories of Friends and Enemies	Selected by Hazel Rochman and Darlene Z. McCampbell	Little Brown and Company
Daring To Be Abigail	Rachel Vail	Puffin
Slot Machine	Chris Lynch	Harper Trophy
Extreme Elvin	Chris Lynch	HarperTrophy
CRASH	Jerry Spinelli	Random House
Wringer	Jerry Spinelli	Harper Trophy
Star Girl	Jerry Spinelli	Knopf
Crazy Lady	Jane Leslie Conly	Harper Trophy
Daphne's Book	Mary Downing Hahn	Camelot
Plague Year	Stephanie S. Tolan	Fawcett Books
Drummers of Jericho	Carolyn Meyer	Harvest Books
Music From a Place Called Half Moon	Jerrie Oughton	Laurel Leaf
Spite Fences	Trudy Krisher	Laurel Leaf
Us and Them: A History of Intolerance in America	Jim Carnes	Oxford Univ. Press Children's Books
Twelve Days in August	Liza Ketchum	Flare. Currently out of print. Look for used on internet
Blue Coyote	Liza Ketchum	Simon and Schuster. Currently out of print. Look for used on Internet

Chapter 2: A Tangle of Emotions
Novels about family relations

TITLE	AUTHOR	PUBLISHER
Plain City	Virginia Hamilton	Scholastic Paperbacks
From the Notebooks of Melanin Sun	Jacqueline Woodson	Scholastic Paperbacks
Belle Prater's Boy	Ruth White	Yearling Books
Zel	Donna Jo Napoli	Puffin
One Bird	Kyoko Mori	Juniper
Tangerine	Edward Bloor	Scholastic Paperbacks
Sons of Liberty	Adele Griffin	Hyperion Press
When I Was Your Age: Original Stories About Growing Up	edited by Amy Ehrlich	Candlewick Press
Following In My Own Footsteps	Mary Downing Hahn	Camelot
Ironman	Chris Crutcher	Laurel Leaf
Kinship	Trudy Krisher	Laurel Leaf
The Great Gilly Hopkins	Katherine Paterson	Harper Trophy
Out of Nowhere	Ouida Sebestyen	Puffin

Chapter 3: When Danger Threatens
Novels about survival

TITLE	AUTHOR	PUBLISHER
Hatchet	Gary Paulsen	Pocket Books
Island of the Blue Dolphin	Scott O'Dell	Scott Foresman
Iceberg Hermit	Arthur Roth	Scholastic Paperbacks
The River	Gary Paulsen	Yearling Books
Brian's Winter	Gary Paulsen	Laurel Leaf
Brian's Return	Gary Paulsen	Laurel Leaf
Guts	Gary Paulsen	Delacorte Press
Dogsong	Gary Paulsen	Pocket Books
The Cay	Theodore Taylor	Random House
Far North	Will Hobbs	Camelot
Downriver	Will Hobbs	Dell Publishing Company
River Thunder	Will Hobbs	Laurel Leaf

The Maze	Will Hobbs	Camelot
Between a Rock and *a* *Hard Place*	Alden R. Carter	Scholastic Paperbacks
Frozen Stiff	Sherry Shahan	Laurel Leaf
The Sacrifice	Diane Matcheck	Penguin Putnam
The Place of Lions	Eric Campbell	Harcourt
Stones in Water	Donna Jo Napoli	Puffin
The Girl Who Owned a City	O. T. Nelson	Runestone Press
River Rats	Caroline Stevermer	Magic Carpet Books
Read for Your Life *Tales of Survival*	Editors of *Read* *Magazine*	Millbrook Press Trade
Tomorrow When the War *Began*	John Marsden	Laurel Leaf
The Dead of Night	John Marsden	Laurel Leaf
A Killing Frost	John Marsden	Laurel Leaf
Darkness Be My Friend	John Marsden	Houghton Mifflin
Burning for Revenge	John Marsden	Houghton Mifflin
The Night Is for Hunting	John Marsden	Houghton Mifflin
The Other Side of Dawn	John Marsden	Houghton Mifflin

Chapter 4: Beyond Stereotypes
Novels about growing up in other cultures

TITLE	AUTHOR	PUBLISHER
Against Borders: *Promoting Books for a* *Multicultural World*	Hazel Rochman	American Library Association Editions
Shabanu	Suzanne Fisher Staples	Random House Children's Publications
Haveli	Suzanne Fisher Staples	Random House Children's Publications
Homeless Bird	Gloria Whelan	Harper Trophy
Against the Storm	Gaye Hiçyilmaz	Yearling Books
A Thief in the Village and *Other Stories of Jamaica*	James Berry	Viking Press
Join In	Donald R. Gallo	Laurel Leaf
For the Life of Laetitia	Merle Hodge	Farrar Straus & Giroux
Among the Volcanoes	Omar S. Castaneda	Yearling Books

Taste of Salt	Frances Temple	Harper Trophy
Go and Come Back	Joan Abelove	Puffin
Broken Bridge	Lynne Reid Banks	Flare
One More River	Lynne Reid Banks	Avon
Habibi	Naomi Shihab Nye	Pocket Books
AK	Peter Dickinson	Laurel Leaf
Chain of Fire	Beverley Naidoo	Harper Trophy
Somehow Tenderness Survives	Hazel Rochman	Harper Trophy
A Girl Named Disaster	Nancy Farmer	Puffin
Thunder Cave	Roland Smith	Disney Press
The Captive	Joyce Hansen	Apple

Chapter 5: No Longer Strangers
Novels about refugees

TITLE	AUTHOR	PUBLISHER
Tonight By Sea	Frances Temple	Harper Trophy
Grab Hands and Run	Frances Temple	Harper Trophy
Lost on Earth: Nomads of the New World	Mark Fritz	Routledge
Journey of the Sparrows	Fran Leeper Buss with the assistance of Daisy Cubias	Puffin
Lupita Manana	Patricia Beatty	Harper Collins Juvenile Books
The Storyteller's Beads	Jane Kurtz	Gulliver Books
The Return	Sonia Levitin	Fawcett Books
Kiss the Dust	Elizabeth Laird	Puffin
The Clay Marble	Minfong Ho	Farrar Straus & Giroux
Goodbye, Vietnam	Gloria Whelan	Random House
Skateway to Freedom	Ann Alma	Beach Holme Publications, Ltd.
Children of the River	Linda Crew	Laurel Leaf
Shadow of the Dragon	Sherry Garland	Harcourt
Thief of Hearts	Lawrence Yep	Harper Trophy
Join In	edited by Donald R. Gallo	Laurel Leaf
The Spirit Catches You and You Fall Down	Anne Fadiman	Farrar Straus & Giroux

Monkey Bridge	Lan Cao	Penguin USA
Arranged Marriages	Chitra Banerjee Divakaruni	Anchor
Interpreter of Maladies	Jhumpa Lahiri	Houghton Mifflin Co.

Chapter 6: Bruised and Outside
Novels about the homeless

TITLE	AUTHOR	PUBLISHER
Slake's Limbo	Felice Holman	Alladdin Paperbacks
No Turning Back	Beverly Naidoo	Harper Trophy
Taste of Salt	Frances Temple	Harper Trophy
The King of Dragons	Carol Fenner	Alladdin Paperbacks
Monkey Island	Paula Fox	Yearling Books
Mary Wolf	Cynthia D. Grant	Simon Pulse
Make Lemonade	Virginia Euwer Wolff	Point
True Believer	Virginia Euwer Wolff	Atheneum
The Planet of Junior Brown	Virginia Hamilton	Pocket Books
The Midwife's Apprentice	Karen Cushman	Harper Trophy
Street Child	Berlie Doherty	Puffin
Jip: His Story	Katherine Paterson	Puffin
Nowhere to Call Home	Cynthia DeFelice	Harper Collins Juvenile Books